Forensic Psychology: A Very Short Introduction

VERY SHORT INTRODUCTIONS are for anyone wanting a stimulating and accessible way in to a new subject. They are written by experts, and have been published in more than 25 languages worldwide.

The series began in 1995, and now represents a wide variety of topics in history, philosophy, religion, science, and the humanities. The VSI Library now contains over 200 volumes—a Very Short Introduction to everything from ancient Egypt and Indian philosophy to conceptual art and cosmology—and will continue to grow to a library of around 300 titles.

Very Short Introductions available now:

For more information visit our web site:
www.oup.co.uk/general/vsi/

David Canter

FORENSIC
PSYCHOLOGY

A Very Short Introduction

OXFORD
UNIVERSITY PRESS

OXFORD

UNIVERSITY PRESS

Great Clarendon Street, Oxford OX2 6DP

Oxford University Press is a department of the University of Oxford.
It furthers the University's objective of excellence in research, scholarship,
and education by publishing worldwide in

Oxford New York

Auckland Cape Town Dar es Salaam Hong Kong Karachi
Kuala Lumpur Madrid Melbourne Mexico City Nairobi
New Delhi Shanghai Taipei Toronto

With offices in

Argentina Austria Brazil Chile Czech Republic France Greece
Guatemala Hungary Italy Japan Poland Portugal Singapore
South Korea Switzerland Thailand Turkey Ukraine Vietnam

Oxford is a registered trade mark of Oxford University Press
in the UK and in certain other countries

Published in the United States
by Oxford University Press Inc., New York

British Library Cataloguing in Publication Data

Data available

Library of Congress Cataloging in Publication Data

Data available

Typeset by SPI Publisher Services, Pondicherry, India
Printed in Great Britain
Ashford Colour Press Ltd, Gosport, Hampshire

ISBN 978-0-19-955020-3

5 7 9 10 8 6 4

Contents

Acknowledgements

I am deeply grateful to my literary representative, Doreen Montgomery of Rupert Crew Ltd, who, as ever, has supported and assisted me in great detail throughout the development of this book and is responsible for at least one hundred commas and many hyphens that would not otherwise be. Michael Davis readily gave of his time and experience as a forensic clinical psychologist to ensure that my account was as accurate as possible. Any errors, and most of the commas, are my sole responsibility.

List of Illustrations

Chapter 1
The excitement and challenge of forensic psychology

Murder, robbery, arson, fraud, domestic violence, child abuse, extortion, rape, and other crimes are the stuff of fact and fiction. They always have been. Even the Bible has murder and fraud in its opening chapters. Yet our fascination with the processes of crime and the law always leads back to attempts to understand and modify the actions of individuals. So although economics, politics, socio-legal studies, and sociology are all of great relevance to the consideration of crime and criminality, at the heart of all crimes are people. These people may be those whose actions constitute the crime, those who attempt to solve it, prosecute it, or to manage the offenders or help their victims. In other words, at every point in the criminal system are psychological processes that need to be addressed. An understanding of these processes and their applications is the basis for forensic psychology.

What is forensic psychology?

As I sit at my desk about to write this *Very Short Introduction*, I have a stack of textbooks, shoulder height, every one of which purports to be about forensic psychology. Yet the contents of one book hardly overlap with the contents of another. Each topic, such as 'offender profiling', 'psychopathy', 'detecting deception', 'treating sex offenders', 'battered woman syndrome', or 'assessing risk of future violence', which is a part of forensic psychology, may be given pride of place in one book but never even find its way into the index in another.

So, I need to be clear from the start. Writing this *Very Short Introduction* is like trying to hit a moving target. Forensic psychology is not what it was, and is fast becoming something other than it is now. Furthermore, somewhat chameleon-like, it cloaks itself in varying guises depending on the legal and socio-cultural setting. What forensic psychologists do also differs markedly from one institutional setting to another. These evolving, variegated forms are what give the whole exploration of the interaction between psychology, crime, and the law an exciting dynamic quality.

For although the term 'forensic' originally meant 'of service to the courts', these days the term 'forensic psychology' is used to cover all aspects of psychology that are relevant to the whole legal and criminal process. It thus runs from:

- explanations of why a person may contemplate committing a crime, and
- the manner of their doing so, through to
- contributions to helping investigate the crime and
- catch the perpetrators, and on to
- providing guidance to those involved in civil and criminal court proceedings
- including the provision of expert testimony about the offender and
- subsequent contributions to the work of prisons and
- other ways of dealing with offenders, especially
- various forms of 'treatment' and rehabilitation.

Sometimes the term 'forensic psychologist' is applied to any psychologist who has anything to do with the police or working with criminals. This would include helping police officers, or those working in prisons, to deal with the stresses of their job or even their selection and management.

Fundamental to these professional activities are a number of psychological issues. These are informed by research and debates that have their roots in general psychology including:

- explanations of the psychological basis of many different forms of offending behaviour and criminality,
- explorations of decision-making and its relevance to the processes of investigating crime,
- studies of the psychology of memory and its bearing on the interviewing of witnesses and suspects,
- consideration of the behavioural and social aspects of court proceedings,
- including the construction of plausible narratives, and
- how juries reach their verdicts,
- the assessment of risk, especially of re-offending, and
- the management of those risks,
- consideration of the viability and effectiveness of rehabilitation processes,
- notably relating to drug and alcohol abuse,
- the role of mental disorder in crime, and
- what leads people to desist from crime.

Forensic psychology is therefore the application to all aspects of the law and management of crime and criminals, through professional practice, of principles, theories, and methods derived from the scientific and clinical studies of human actions and experience. It thus also has a strong academic research strand that is concerned notably with the psychology of offending. Conceptually, as a consequence, forensic psychology sits between criminology, forensic psychiatry, and jurisprudence, drawing also on other disciplines as diverse as socio-legal studies; human geography; clinical, developmental, and social psychology; and psychometrics.

For those completely new to this area, it may need to be explained that psychiatry is a medical speciality with a strong focus on mental illness. Psychologists do not normally have any medical qualifications, studying human actions and experiences as a scientific discipline. Some psychologists go on to specialize in working with people who are mentally disturbed. Such psychologists are typically called 'clinical psychologists', and work

1. Hugo Munsterberg, who wrote one of the first forensic psychology books, titled *On the Witness Stand: Essays on Psychology and Crime*

with psychiatrists and other mental health professionals. So there is a distinction between practitioners of forensic psychology and forensic psychiatry. The latter are fundamentally medical doctors, who have the right to prescribe medicines; the former derive their central contributions from the social and behavioural sciences.

The distinction between forensic psychology and criminology is possibly the most difficult for those outside these disciplines to understand. Further confusion is caused by the fact that in the United States the overlap between these two areas is much greater than in the United Kingdom. Additional misunderstanding can be caused by the use of terms such as 'criminalistics' and 'criminal psychology'.

Put as simply as possible, criminology is the study of *crime*. It emphasizes social causes, patterns, developments, and ways of reducing crime. By contrast, forensic psychology is the study of *criminals*. So although, for example, many forensic psychologists may accept that levels of poverty are an important influence on crime rates, they would not study such a relationship in the way criminologists would. Rather, forensic psychologists would be concerned more directly with why some people in poverty commit crimes and others do not. In this book, then, we will not concern ourselves with crime rates or other aspects of the sociology of crime, as important as these obviously are.

One final distinction is worth mentioning. This is the difference between forensic psychology and forensic science. The latter grows out of chemistry, toxicology, physics, pathology, and the other natural sciences. Although I have been asked by lawyers who did not know the difference to carry out a medical examination of a rape victim, that would be outside my competence as a behavioural scientist, as would be an autopsy, or testing for poisons in a blood sample; all of these are aspects of forensic pathology and forensic science.

Where did forensic psychology come from?

For as long as there has been any form of psychology, it has been used both to explain criminality and to propose methods for managing criminals and reducing crime. The implacable presence of crime in all societies throughout history, and the frequent failure of most attempts at crime reduction, probably says as much about the inherent nature of criminality in being human as it does about the weaknesses in our understanding of criminality.

In modern times, however, the opening for psychological involvement in the legal process is usually linked to the case of Daniel McNaughton. He was convicted of killing Edward Drummond, whom he shot on 20 January 1843. Drummond actually died from complications a few days after McNaughton shot him, the wound itself apparently not being very severe. The significance of this murder was that the killer is reported to have said in his defence:

> The Tories in my native city have compelled me to do this. They follow and persecute me wherever I go, and have entirely destroyed my peace of mind.

This was taken to indicate that he had persecutory delusions and had intended to kill Sir Robert Peel, the leader of the Tory party, mistakenly killing Drummond, who was Peel's private secretary.

In the 1840s, there was no clear defence of insanity, merely a general requirement that the culprit knew what he or she was doing and knew it to be wrong. This is encapsulated in the legal term *mens rea*, which indicates that the offender must have had some conscious agency that gave rise to the criminal acts. If a person is so mentally disturbed that he or she is not really aware that the action will have criminal consequences, then in most

Forensic Psychology

6

CENTRAL CRIMINAL COURT, OLD BAILEY—M'NAUGHTEN'S TRIAL.

2. The trial of Daniel McNaughton

civilized jurisdictions there is a preference for treating the person rather than punishing him or her. But when this defence was used to find Daniel McNaughton 'not guilty on the ground of insanity', there was a public outcry, in which Queen Victoria herself participated. This led to a clarification of the insanity defence that required, crucially, the demonstration that the accused had a 'disease of the mind' at the time of the offence that limited his or her ability to know that what he or she was doing and/or that it was wrong. These criteria became known as the 'McNaughton Rules'.

The reference in law to a 'disease of the mind' implies some medical illness, as if the mind were an organ that could be infected or become sick like the liver or the lungs. There is no simple equation here between the mind and the brain. A person may have any of a number of brain diseases without losing the ability to tell right from wrong. There are also plenty of forms of mental illness for which no apparent disease of the brain can be identified. So specifying a 'disease of the mind' opened the way to a great variety of quasi-medical and non-medical examinations of suspects to determine whether they could plead insanity.

Laboratory-based, experimental psychologists found their way into court as experts by a rather different route. Drawing on studies of perception and memory, they have been able to comment on disputed testimony and challenged statements from witnesses. Early examples were the contributions of Hugo Munsterberg, such as his defence of Flemish weavers. Their customer had complained that the cloth supplied was not the colour of what had been ordered. Munsterberg was able to show that the disagreement was because of variations in perception under differing lighting conditions.

The recognition that there were psychological processes that needed to be understood and dealt with as part of criminal investigations and court proceedings slowly evolved to encompass many other aspects of criminality and the law. Psychologists increasingly drew on a wide range of theories and methodologies to contribute to the court's deliberations. Following Munsterberg and others, the understanding of remembering provided the basis for expert evidence on what witnesses may or may not have been able to remember. Those who had studied educational processes or family relationships would comment on children and give guidance in family courts on issues of parental custody. Indeed, once psychological contributions to legal processes had been allowed into court, then just about any area of professional or academic psychology could be drawn upon to contribute to the management of criminals and the consequences of their actions. Therefore, today, many of the activities of forensic psychologists are far removed from the debate that Daniel McNaughton initiated when he said he was persecuted by the Tories.

Where does forensic psychology happen?

Despite over one hundred years of wide-ranging psychological contributions to legal issues, the medical framework still dominates legal considerations of defendants' mental states. 'Battered wife syndrome', 'post-traumatic stress disorder', 'rape trauma syndrome', and a number of other summaries of people's actions and experiences are couched in what seem like medical terminology, in part, at least, to make them acceptable to the courts. Initially, then, as mentioned, it is not surprising that most of the evidence about mental states was given in court by people with medical qualifications, even if they were drawing on psychological assessments made by other people. So, for the first hundred years or so after Edward Drummond was shot, there was no strong forensic psychology presence in most jurisdictions.

Today, however, forensic psychology spreads much wider than the pseudo-medical labelling of offenders and their actions. It is perhaps best understood in terms of its applications to a number of rather different areas of professional practice: the investigation and apprehension of offenders; the processes of trial and decisions in court; management and attempts at rehabilitation in prison and other institutional settings, or in the community – all relating to the fundamental question of what gives rise to criminality. We will therefore consider this central issue in Chapter 2.

Psychology in court

With the widespread development of psychology in many walks of life, stimulated by the use of psychologists during the Second World War and the burgeoning psychology industry in the USA, from the middle of the 20th century legal opinions about a defendant's mental processes and personality were increasingly provided by psychologists who had no medical qualifications. Yet the medical influence was still strong. In the UK, at least, initially those psychologists who did provide guidance to the courts tended to be clinical psychologists who worked with mental patients. Forensic psychology was a speciality within the postgraduate speciality of clinical psychology, and that clinical tradition is still very strong.

However, once psychologists got their foot in the door of the courtroom, the way was open for a much wider range of applications than merely commenting on the *mens rea* of the accused. Increasingly, the courts, and others working with criminals, looked to psychologists for a wider assessment of the offender. They sought help in understanding the implications of the crime, and the most appropriate way of dealing with the offender. This spread to cover more direct assessment of the dangerousness of offenders and other psychological issues in which the legal process had an interest.

This involvement of psychology has broadened even further so that nowadays issues as varied as the reliability of witness testimony or the selection of juries are all dealt with by psychologists, many of whom are far removed from clinical considerations, or any direct involvement with individual offenders as their clients. In part because of the readiness of the US courts to allow experts to testify and the entrepreneurial approach to setting up independent consultancies, this form of legal advice on witnesses and juries is a dominant aspect of forensic psychology in the USA.

Chapter 3 reviews the contributions that forensic psychologists make as expert witnesses. Chapter 4 examines the broader issues of psychological contributions to the legal process.

Psychology in forensic treatment settings

The early psychological advice about the mental state of offenders tended to be an outcrop of the assessment and treatment of offenders who were deemed to have mental or personality problems. So that, in fact, the settings in which forensic psychology had its roots were those variety of institutions that provide treatment for offenders. Some are known in the UK as 'special hospitals', or in the USA by the euphemism of 'correctional establishments'. Both of these are part of the prison system, but often place greater emphasis on trying to change the person's behaviour than the punishment focus of many prisons. Many more conventional clinical treatment settings may also have offenders as patients, helping them, for example, to deal with their addictions, or their aggression, or indeed their traumas.

Psychology in the prison and probation service

Work in special hospitals and other clinical settings spilled over into prisons, and from there into the follow-up in probation services. A distinct prison and probation psychology (often referred to in the USA as 'correctional psychology') is emerging as a response to this, producing a discrete speciality over the last quarter of a century. It seems to be strongest in those countries that have centralized, or government-controlled, prison systems and integrated probation services, such as Australia, the UK, and Italy.

These services have developed very rapidly in these and other countries over the past decade, moving far beyond the assessments of intelligence and reviews of personality on which many forensic psychologists focused half a century ago. There are now many areas on which they will produce reports about prisoners, whether at the early stages of their incarceration to help guide their progress through prison, or assessing risk and other matters of interest to a parole board, and at various stages along the way and after they leave prison. This may not always be welcomed by prisoners, of course, who may feel that their freedom within prison may be curtailed by what the 'trick cyclist' has to say about them.

Beyond reporting on individuals, though, psychologists in prisons are likely to draw on many other areas of behavioural science.

This includes evaluations of prison programmes and regimes, helping to plan organizational change and training staff in various approaches that may help to reduce further offending. As a consequence, many prison and probation psychologists are more comfortable with the label 'applied psychologist' rather than 'forensic psychologist'.

Chapter 5 provides an overview of the work that psychologists carry out with offenders.

Psychology and investigations

The most popularly known activity of forensic psychologists is their contribution to police investigations. This is probably due more to the apparent need for a modern-day Sherlock Holmes in most crime fiction than to any prevalence in fact. Graced with the somewhat misleading label of 'offender profiler', these clever, but usually flawed, fictional characters are portrayed as seeing into the criminal's mind to help the police solve the case. The crimes are almost invariably some form of serial killing, and the 'profiler' seems to have the uncanny ability of knowing what the murderer thinks and feels. These insights appear to be based on little more than the crime scene and other odds and ends of clues.

As the person usually credited with bringing offender profiling to the UK, apparently in a parcel from the FBI in Virginia, I despair every time a journalist asks me for a 'profile' of the unknown criminal whose actions are in the day's news. This has become an area in which myth and fiction combine to hide the often rather mundane truth to such a degree that I have to take a deep breath and say as gently as I can, 'it's not like on TV you know'.

It is true that there are results emerging from the study of criminal behaviour that can contribute to the search for unknown offenders. But this is far removed from 'getting into the mind' of the criminal. It is much more to do with improving police decision-making processes by enabling them to draw on a wide range of psychological discoveries. This has been most significant in the development of police-interviewing techniques, particularly with helping witnesses to remember more details.

In so far as psychology contributes directly to suggesting useful offender characteristics, this is more likely to be about where the offender may be based or how he or she may be found in police records. This is much more useful than speculations about his or her mental processes, although these were the sorts of comments that were made in the early days of profiling in the middle of the last century. Then, the dominant medical framework meant that early 'profiles' were actually generated by people who had a special interest in criminals who were mentally ill. Although their contributions are often written about in a heroic light (not unusually by the 'profilers' themselves), close analysis reveals that they were hardly ever of real and direct value to the investigation.

As I will explore further in Chapter 6, I have been at pains to put some distance between the contributions psychologists can make to investigations and the pseudo-heroic deeds of 'profilers'. I coined the term 'investigative psychology' to distinguish this area of psychology. A number of police forces around the world have followed this lead and have set up investigative psychology units that contribute much more to the work of law enforcement than the early 'profilers' ever did.

So although forensic psychology is still a young discipline, it has already spun off a number of subdisciplines. Prison psychology, investigative psychology, legal psychology, and forensic aspects of clinical psychology are all emerging as rather distinct areas of study and professional activity. There have also been a number of areas in which psychology has made a notable impact, perhaps most strongly in assisting police-interviewing techniques and reducing the number of miscarriages of justice. There is also growing evidence that psychology can be of help in enabling some criminals to move away from a life of crime.

Challenges to forensic psychology

Forensic psychology is probably one of the fastest growing areas of professional psychology around the world, in part because of the attractive myth of offender profiling and the widespread interest in crime and criminals. Yet this mushrooming growth must be set against a backdrop of the remarkable difficulties of carrying out proper studies in this area and the many challenges practitioners face. Access to real criminals or juries for research purposes, or to witnesses or police officers, is always fraught with legal and practical constraints. In some cases, there are also real dangers that need to be planned for and avoided. Therefore much research of relevance to forensic psychology, notably on eyewitness testimony, has been carried out in rather artificial settings, often consisting of scenarios that can be somewhat unrealistic, in which students are shown videos then requested to indicate what they remember. This has rather limited applicability outside of the laboratory because it is based on simulations, with people drawn from a limited subset of the population who are under no real pressure.

Even work directly with offenders in prisons has many limitations because of the unusual, captive environment in which the studies are carried out and the offenders' separation from their usual social setting. For example, it is very difficult to help people deal with their own abuse of alcohol in a context in which there is no alcohol available and when the degree to which they are participating voluntarily is difficult to gauge. Indeed, some authorities will not allow any research on prisoners because they say an incarcerated person can never give voluntary, informed consent.

There is also the profound challenge of what to believe of what a convict says in any research interview or treatment programme. Usually, in most research or therapeutic situations, the psychologist can work from the assumption that participants are trying to help and will generally be honest in what they say. They may not wish to talk about certain topics, or be confused or traumatized about what they remember, but it would not be expected that they would actively distort, mislead, or lie about themselves and their actions. Inevitably when dealing with offenders, that is exactly the expectation that may be the starting point for any contact. The skill of the psychologist is in moving beyond that to get the truth of the matter, often by using special questionnaires and other procedures for detecting distortions in the accounts they are given.

However, an increasing number of intrepid researchers are overcoming these challenges, working directly and openly with offenders and others involved in law enforcement and the legal process. Such studies are revealing just how complex is criminality and how limited is our understanding of the psychological processes that underlie it. Of particular importance is the diversity of criminals. No two people convicted of similar crimes are identical. As a consequence, there is no simple, standard 'profile' of a burglar or a murderer, or of a terrorist. Offenders themselves will also develop and change psychologically over time. These changes may even be brought about by their experiences of committing crimes. Therefore we cannot assume that we can understand the psychology of a criminal because they have been assigned to the category of bank robber or rapist.

A further complexity is the mixture of crimes that most criminals commit. In popular mythology, serial offending is usually associated with violent crime, especially serial killing. But many offenders commit a large variety of offences throughout the time that they are actively criminal. Although there may be some emphasis on fraud or violence, stealing cars or robbing banks, it is relatively rare to find offenders who are out and out specialists, indulging in only one specific type of crime. There is also a small but fascinating subset of offenders who have lived apparently blameless lives except for one crime, which may be as serious as murder.

In all these complexities a central hurdle to any forensic psychology research keeps re-emerging: being absolutely clear what crime actually is. What is acceptable in one subculture may be outlawed in another. For example, in many countries actions within a marriage are tolerated which would be regarded as rape somewhere else. Therefore the legal definition of offending actions may not always have particular psychological clarity. In dealing with offenders, therefore, psychologists need to get to grips with what they have actually done, rather than what they are legally convicted of. Often forensic psychologists will even wish to put aside the crime that has brought the person to them as a client and try and look more fully at his or her lifestyle and personal situation.

This direct exploration of the psychology of criminals, who are often dealt with as clients in some sort of therapeutic context, is showing how important it is to go beyond fictional accounts of criminals and the notions of 'motives'. Although a person's actions in a burglary, robbery, or a commercial fraud may have the appearance of being driven by the desire for direct financial gain, close consideration often reveals quite other processes. For example, why might a burglar defecate on the bed in the house he burgles? Why does one robber take a gun and another keep well clear of firearms? What is a fraudster seeking to achieve who draws no personal benefit from the money he has illegally obtained? These questions can take us far beyond the limited 'motives' such as greed or revenge that populate crime fiction. The much more subtle task is to determine how offenders see themselves and their roles in relation to their criminal actions.

Bridging cultures

As forensic psychologists moved out from the shelter of medicine, they developed ways of thinking about people that tends to separate them from how lawyers and judges and the police construe their clients or potential suspects. Psychologists often locate the explanation of crime in processes outside of the control of the offender, in genetic make-up, hormones, upbringing, or social experiences. In none of these explanations is much emphasis given to a person making the decision to do something wrong. In contrast, the law sees the responsibility of the offender as paramount. *Mens rea* is the focus of legal enquiry when the culprit is being examined.

These differences in fundamental concerns translate into rather different processes for assessing offenders. Psychologists will typically base their views on trends across people, drawing out underlying dimensions along which people differ, or assigning individuals to 'types' or diagnostic categories. The courts, on the other hand, are appropriately focused on the person in front of them. The discussion is about that particular individual, his or her actions and experiences. Any generalities that the courts draw upon are required to relate directly to the case in front of them.

An illustration of this difference between scientific psychological procedures and the legal process is one case in which I challenged the claims of an apparent expert in linguistics. He was appearing for the defence, saying that his techniques revealed that the confession presented to the court had been produced by more than one person, and thus could be regarded as a fraudulent invention of the police. As psychologists, I and a number of other people had carried out careful studies of the techniques he used with examples of material that was authored by one person or by more than one. These studies showed that the techniques used by this expert had no validity at all. However, for the court I had to show that this general weakness in the techniques, and claims derived from them, could also be demonstrated to be a weakness in the case in question. Our earlier results made this specific, further demonstration scientifically pointless and totally predictable, but it had to be done for the court nonetheless.

In many ways, the central challenges and excitement of forensic psychology come from this interplay between the two very different disciplines of psychology and the law; when effectively working together, they can help each other. Each can move the other beyond the limits of their own professional constraints, and the consequence is one of mutual enrichment.

Chapter 2

How to make a criminal

Are criminals different?

Explanations of criminal behaviour and criminality are central to forensic psychology. These provide the basis for considerations of how criminals can be assessed, whether and how they can be helped to avoid future criminality or be 'treated' in some way. If it is assumed that there is something inherent in being a criminal, then assessment, punishment, and treatment would focus directly on the characteristics of the offender. By contrast, if it is assumed that offenders are created by circumstances, then programmes to reduce crime would focus on those circumstances rather than the individual offender. As a consequence, debates about the causes of crime, which may seem rather abstract, can and do have direct influence on policies for tackling crime and managing offenders.

At the heart of these discussions is the question of whether criminals are different in some fundamental ways from people who have not committed any crime. Is there something about how they are made that distinguishes them? One way of exploring this is to consider what you would have to do to construct a criminal.

Biological explanations

Assume you are a modern-day Dr Frankenstein and you were commissioned to build a criminal. What would you need to complete the task? Would it be particular body parts? Perhaps, as was believed by serious scholars less than one hundred years ago, you would go for especially lengthy arms (like those of apes)? Would you also follow the guidelines of the well-known 19th-century Italian criminologist Ceasare Lombroso in building the head, making sure that it had 'projecting ears, thick hair, a thin beard, enormous jaws, a square and projecting chin and large cheek-bones'? To go further with Victorian ideas of what distinguished criminals from the population at large, you might wish to make sure that yours was below average height, or above, they should also be heavier than non-criminals, or distinctly lighter. If you were following these guidelines, you would also ensure that the criminal you built was pigeon-breasted, with an imperfectly developed chest and stooping shoulders. He would be flat-footed too. (The great majority of detected crimes are committed by men, so from here I will stick with this gender-specific reference for criminals for simplicity, and indicate if I particularly want to consider female criminals.)

If this all sounds too anatomical for you, but you think you could take a normal body and just fiddle with the hormones, genetic make-up, and other aspects of how the body works to create a criminal, you would be in somewhat more up-to-date company. There are plenty of experts who think that criminality is a product of some brain disorder, or even minor brain damage, say as the result of an accident, or problems at the time of birth. For example, recent research has suggested that Henry VIII turned from a benign king at peace with his wife to a despotic ruler who got rid of wives like old shirts after he had a jousting accident that left him unconscious for two hours. It is claimed that the brain damage suffered in the accident changed his personality to become more aggressive and violent.

TYPES DE CRIMINELS

Pl. VI

P. R. Voleur napolitain

B. S. Faussaire Piemontais

BOGGIA assassin

CARTOUCHE

G. MARINI Femme de brigand

DESRUES empoisonneur

Turin, Lith. Salussolia

Forensic Psychology

3. Pictures taken from Lombroso's 1871 *Atlas of Criminal Types*

If it were thought that the cause of rape or murder related to some neurological aspect of the person, then assessment of the offender would search out these aspects. Such an examination would at the very least raise questions about any childhood trauma, especially injuries to the head, or use brain scans or similar explorations of brain function. Some of those who pursue this line of thought even suggest that potential criminals could be identified before they offend by study of their brains.

Some take this biological argument a stage further, claiming that there are deep-seated constituents of criminals' genetics, reflected in such features as an extra Y chromosome. Hormonal imbalances have also been accused. A popular suggestion here is to blame testosterone, the especially male hormone. Nervous systems that do not allow criminals to learn effectively are posited as another cause. The idea is that because criminals are not so responsive to reward and punishment, they never internalize socially acceptable behaviour in the way the law-abiding public does.

The central assumption here is that there is something about the actual, physiological and/or neurological make-up of a person that causes him to become a criminal. This was the central belief in the late 19th century, when the scientific community was overawed by Darwin's theory of evolution as the explanation for everything. Based on rather simplified ideas of the evolutionary process, there was a common scholarly view that criminals were, in essence, a less highly evolved form of humanity. That was why the longer limbs, jutting jaw, and other characteristics that were thought of as evolutionary throwbacks were seen as distinct signs of criminality. Many of the writings of this period refer to criminals as having much in common with children and 'savages', as a further indication that they were not fully evolved human beings.

These sorts of ideas have certainly not gone away. They may take on a more sophisticated vocabulary and hide their basic assumptions in an overlay of biogenetic theory, and reference to the evolution of human behaviour, but the essential idea that criminals are different from other people is inherent in many discussions of the causes of crime. For example, some experts have taken these notions to the extreme of claiming that crimes such as rape and murder are part of man's (and possibly not woman's) evolutionary origins and are therefore hard-wired, as they say, into the human genome.

The implication seems to be that these horrific crimes give some evolutionary benefit in 'the battle for survival'. They therefore continue to exist within modern man because those who committed such acts in the early stages of human evolution were more likely to live on to mate and thus pass on their genes to subsequent generations. This does not really explain, though, why all men are not rapists and murderers. Presumably those who are have to be thought of as closer to their animal origins, or have less control over their atavistic instincts, than those of us who are more virtuous. Such an argument is not very far removed from Lombroso highlighting the small forehead and long arms as indicators of the 'savage' nature of criminals.

These pseudo-evolutionary ideas can be generalized to explain all forms of human aggression. Animals that are prepared to fight when attacked are assumed to be more likely to survive to father new offspring than those that cower or run away. Or, in a rather more Rambo-style interpretation, such aggressive heroes may be more likely to attract one or more mates. Therefore everything from violence at football matches to world wars is put down to our animal instincts.

The problems with all these generalized theories are that they do not make clear why some people, football crowds, nations, and epochs are typically peaceful, whilst others make aggression their hallmark. If aggression is a fundamental component of man's genetic inheritance, why do all men not exhibit this trait across all locations and time periods? Any answer has to imply that there is something about the particular constituents of that person, crowd, or country that makes them either more or less likely to express their aggressive instincts. In other words, evolutionary explanations, if they are valid at all, provide only a broadly painted backdrop to what makes us human. It is rather like saying that a lot of criminality emerges out of the fact that nearly all criminals have two arms and two legs and therefore walk, run, and often climb.

The crucial questions are about what leads particular individuals to draw on those aspects of being human, that we all share, to commit crimes? Explanations are required that deal with the origins of criminal activities in subsets of individuals, particular groups, or nations, or eras, rather than a product of the evolution of the whole human species. So we return to the question of whether criminals really are different from the rest of humanity.

One, admittedly cynical, way of considering these attempts at biological or evolutionary explanations of criminality is perhaps to see them as part of a turf war between different professional disciplines. They are a way that biologically orientated psychologists and psychiatrists can claim 'ownership' of the problem of criminality. They can say 'leave it to us, we have the answer'. This is a battle over who has the best insights into offending, in which many different disciplines engage. Yet, as we shall see, criminality is so much part of being human that no one discipline can ever claim a monopoly over understanding it.

Many psychologists argue that the idea that offenders are different from non-offenders does not need to assume profound biological differences between them and the population at large. There can be a variety of more directly personal reasons why people could end up being a part of a distinct subset. So, in making a criminal you might decide to take a much easier option and instead of trying to manufacture a criminal from scratch, drawing only on physical and neurological constituents, you would select people who you thought would become criminal. What would you look for? Well, if you were to draw on the general descriptions offered for the average offender, you might select people of lower than average intelligence, who were rather impulsive and somewhat neurotic, but who yearned for excitement.

The difficulty you might run into with any of these anatomical, biological, or psychological approaches to making a criminal would be that you may just end up with a person who is indistinguishable from many non-criminal individuals. Indeed, some of the characteristics that you are drawing on may offer the basis for people who become famous footballers or even politicians. It is necessary to go beyond the broad characteristics of offenders and to look more closely at the mental processes that may possibly underlie criminality.

Mental disorder

One way of handling the challenge posed by how few people, typically, are criminal even though an evolutionary perspective may suggest that all men might be expected to be, is to look for some breakdown in normal functioning, some lever in the person's mechanism that has come loose, been bent or disturbed in some way. The source of such disturbance would be in mental processes, so it is various aspects of mental disorder that are often explored to explain criminality.

It is certainly not uncommon to find offenders suffering from some form of depression, or have learning disabilities, or even a psychotic condition such as schizophrenia. Indeed, in one study of men in English prisons it was found that as many as three in every hundred were severely psychotic; that is what many people would simply call 'mad'—a lack of contact with reality, such as hearing voices, having hallucinations, or believing that some secret force was controlling their lives. There is also a curious group we need to look at separately who are assigned the rather intriguing diagnosis of having a disordered 'personality', or even more generally, 'antisocial personality disorder'. So there are certainly plenty of criminals who suffer from various forms of mental problems. This will consequently be of relevance when considering how they commit their crimes and what to do with them when arrested and convicted. But whether the proportion in a sample of criminals is any larger than in the population from which offenders are drawn is a moot point. Furthermore, whether the lifestyles of criminals and their experiences of incarceration may be the cause of their mental problems, as opposed to the mental disorder causing them to be criminal, is often hard to disentangle.

There are a number of difficulties in accepting mental disorder as a cause of criminal acts. Even though certain acts of violence, such as the murder of wife and children, may relate to the perpetrator being depressed, most certainly not all depressed people commit crimes. Further, despite newspapers being ready to mention that a killer had been diagnosed as schizophrenic, in fact the vast majority of psychotic individuals, whether they are paranoid or not, are far more danger to themselves than ever to anyone else. This is not to be confused with the finding that schizophrenics are more likely than those without that diagnosis to be violent, especially if they take drugs. The prevalence of schizophrenics who commit crimes is still very low, and the question also arises as to whether their crimes, especially violence, are a reaction to how they are treated rather than being directly caused by their illness.

People with learning difficulties are by their nature more dependent on those around them for guidance and support than the population at large. Therefore, people with these intellectual difficulties will most likely offend if that is what their upbringing and surroundings have encouraged them to do. It is doubtful that their learning difficulties are the sole cause of their offending.

There is thus an important difference between being a mentally disordered offender and mental disorder causing offending. There is a need to take seriously the prevalence of mental disorder in populations of convicted men and women because this does provide a rather distinct area of professional intervention for forensic psychologists. Just as in the population at large, those with mental disorders can benefit from various forms of therapy, so in the offending population there will be plenty of people who need help to deal with their psychological problems. Their criminal activity may well complicate the possibilities for dealing with these mental problems, but it can fall to the lot of psychologists who are part of forensic services to provide the needed assistance.

Psychopathy and beyond

There are many individuals who commit crimes who understand perfectly what they do and its illegality but who have no obvious mental problems. They are lucid and coherent with no signs of any learning disability or psychotic symptoms. Some of them can be superficially charming and are intelligent enough to be very plausible on first acquaintance. They do not hear voices or think that they are commanded by forces beyond their power to commit crimes. Yet, over and over again, they abuse people, lie without any compunction or remorse, can be unpredictably violent, and seem unable to relate effectively to others over any extended period. Various forms of criminality are almost inevitably an aspect of the lifestyles of these individuals. In the jargon of mental health professionals, such people may be given a diagnosis that implies that their 'personality' is somehow disordered.

In psychiatric medicalization of human activity, a whole set of 'personality disorders' has been identified that attempts to distinguish different ways in which individuals may have difficulty in relating to others. The one that has found its way into popular discourse is 'psychopathic disorder'. There are complications here because the term 'psychopathic disorder' is not a medical diagnosis but a legal term under English and Welsh law that refers to a 'persistent disorder or disability of the mind', not that far removed from the McNaughton rule that first emerged over a century and a half ago. Thus there is some debate as to which of the psychiatric diagnoses of personality disorder are closest to the legal definition of 'psychopathic disorder', and whether any of them relates to the popular conception of a psychopath.

The Hollywood portrayal of the psychopath is someone who is inevitably a merciless serial killer, often some sort of cross between Dracula and Frankenstein's monster. Silent films from the 1920s such as *The Cabinet of Dr Caligari* to the more recent *Kalifornia*, or *No Country for Old Men*, never really provide any psychological insights into the actions of the monsters who are the anti-heroes of their dramas. They are presented as pure evil. The rather more psychologically interesting films such as *Psycho* or *The Boston Strangler* provide pseudo-Freudian explanations for the nastiness of their villains, but still present them as rather alien individuals who can appear unthreatening but deep down are malevolent.

Until you have met someone whom you know has committed horrific violent crimes but can be charming and helpful, it is difficult to believe in the Hollywood stereotype of the psychopath. Without doubt, there are people who can seem pleasant and plausible in one situation but can quickly turn to viciousness. There are also people who just never connect with others and are constantly, from an early age, at war with those with whom they come into contact. If we need a label for these people, we can distinguish them as type 1 and type 2 psychopaths. The former have superficial charm, are pathological liars, being callous and manipulative. The clearest fictional example of this sort of psychopath is Tom Ripley, who has the central role in many of Patricia Highsmith's amoral novels. The type 2 psychopaths are more obviously criminal, impulsive, and irresponsible with a history of juvenile delinquency and early behavioural problems.

4. Is the disgraced financier Bernard Madoff a psychopath?

5. Or is the Hannibal Lector character portrayed by Anthony Hopkins a more accurate example?

Another label that may be assigned to people who are habitually involved in illegal, reckless, and remorseless activities that has a much broader net than 'psychopathy' is 'antisocial personality disorder'. But we should not be seduced into thinking that these diagnoses are anything other than summary descriptions of the people in question. They do not help us to understand the causes of people behaving in these unacceptable ways. Some experts have even commented that they are actually moral judgements masquerading as medical explanations. So although the labels 'personality disorder' and 'psychopath' do summarize useful descriptions of some rather difficult, and often nasty, people, we need to look elsewhere for explanations of how they come to be like that.

DSM and ICD

The labels to describe mentally ill offenders are derived from worthy attempts to impose a form of medically precise diagnoses on the mix of actions and thoughts that characterize some criminals. Two approaches to classification dominate these considerations. One is produced, and revised regularly, by the American Psychiatric Association and is known as the Diagnostic and Statistical Manual of Mental Disorders, having reached a text revised version of its fourth edition, so DSM-IV-TR. The other is the mental disorders section of the International Classification of Diseases and Related Health Problems, usually abbreviated to the International Classification of Diseases, which is in its tenth edition, hence ICD-10.

These classification schemes are widely drawn upon, especially in legal proceedings, despite their authors being at pains to warn against their use in court. They are nonetheless used because they give a framework, or useful shorthand, for typifying bundles of features of a person. Fitting individuals into the classifications on offer can sometimes feel like nailing jelly to the wall. The classifications deal with complex and changing aspects of how people interact with others and live their lives. They do not identify particular bacteria or damage to distinct parts of the brain.

Addiction and substance abuse

One common explanation for crime is that it is caused by the abuse of alcohol or drugs, or addiction to illegal substances. Could you make your criminal by getting them addicted? It is certainly the case that some aspects of the activity of criminals are influenced by various forms of intoxication. They may be more violent and impulsive when under the influence. Their actions may have a less obvious logic to them and be less effective, like the offender who ram-raided a shop, but chose a pound shop rather than a jeweller's. In addition, the maintenance of criminal activity may be a consequence of the inability to shed an addiction.

There is the need to find funds to purchase the addictive substances, so people can be kept in such a state of dependency for their drug-supply that they continue to offend to obtain the money to buy the drugs. The illegality of many substances and their use also creates a criminal milieu in the way that alcohol prohibition did in the United States in the 1930s. So people can drift into criminal actions because of their use and dealings in drugs.

But addiction can never be the whole explanation of why people commit crimes. Many people finance their addictions from legitimate sources. Furthermore, many established criminals drift into the use of drugs only when their criminal activity generates enough money to enable them to afford these drugs.

Addiction is certainly an important aspect of the lifestyle of many criminals. Like mental disorder, it presents another area in which forensic psychologists are called upon to help offenders. Assisting men and women to come off drugs can be an important step in getting them to develop a non-criminal lifestyle. But drug addiction on its own is not the cause of crime. In combination with other psychological problems, nonetheless, it can contribute to a potent spiral that leads to crime.

Psychological explanations

Perhaps the most direct way of finding someone who is likely to make a criminal is to look for someone who does not accept the usual social mores. In popular parlance, we might expect such a person not to have developed much of a conscience. A more technical, psychological description would be to claim that the person had not reached the adult stage of moral reasoning. Although this has curious throwbacks to the 19th-century idea that criminals were close to 'children and savages', at least it gives a more detailed framework for considering the cognitive processes of offenders. It also opens up a way of exploring what it is about people who are labelled 'psychopaths' that contributes to their acting as they do.

Such explanations are thus part of a family of psychological theories that consider criminality to be rooted in ways of making sense of the world. These run a gamut of aspects of a person's mental life including:

- lack of awareness of the consequence of any actions, especially of the people who will suffer those consequences, supported by
- justifications of criminal actions and attempts to claim that their impact is minimal
- low feelings of self-worth that are reduced by criminal success,
- rational assessment that crime 'pays', based on the belief that offending provides high rewards for little effort,
- a general unwillingness to delay gratification, or
- the inability to control desires.

Putting these various theories together can be most readily understood as three psychological stages that give rise to offending behaviour.

- The first is the interpretation of the situation. This may be erroneous, with others' gestures and comments being misattributed, as in the often-heard precursor to violence 'Who are you looking at?' Or it may be a reasonably accurate understanding of what is going on, but the situation is taken as one for which a criminal response is deemed appropriate.
- This takes the offender into the second stage, in which a mixture of emotions and habitual reactions give rise to the offence. An open window may be interpreted as an opportunity for burglary, a snub in a pub as a reason for violence, or a more thought-through bank robbery can evolve out of discussions about the opportunities available.
- The final stage is also the crucial lack of any real concern for the consequences of the crime.

These three stages each draw attention to characteristics of the person and how they typically react in various situations – what psychologists call their 'personality'. A number of researchers emphasize the neurotic extrovert personalities of many criminals. However, there are also aspects of upbringing and social background that are inherent in all three stages. For example, if a person rarely suffers the consequences of his actions, then he may be expected to be less concerned with them. If he grows up in a subculture in which violence is always just below the surface, then hitting out may be more part of his social repertoire than talking things through.

A further possibility is that a person's characteristics, whilst not inherently criminal, may make him more vulnerable to drifting into offending. So, although there are doubtless aspects of some people that make them more likely to be criminal, this may be more a feature, for example, of their difficulty in coping with school

33

or social relationships. Their difficulties may be in being unable to survive as law-abiding citizens because their particular social group expects them to offend. All of these aspects of a person's situation may contribute to their offending rather than this being some inherent evil with which they are born.

Social explanations

The view that criminals are different from everyone else contrasts with the approach which sees that we could all be criminal in the right circumstances. This therefore leads to the view that it is not within the person that explanations for crime should be sought, but in their circumstances. This is a slightly different approach to understanding crime from the biological, medical ones we have been considering. It is a step further on from explanations inherent in personal psychology, but one that runs into problems similar to those found in individually orientated explanations.

In a serious and worthy attempt to deal with criminality in Victorian times, a number of reformers, driven by the Christian principle that all human beings are equal, believed strongly that criminality was a product of contact with other criminals. In the 20th century, this idea was graced with the title of 'association theory'. The argument was that by growing up in a criminal environment, especially a criminal family, the individual would learn the habits and indeed the skills of being criminal. From this perspective, the psychological processes we have considered could, in the main, be seen to have their origins in families that, for example, did not teach their children to delay gratification, which never gave them any feeling of self-esteem, and only regarded success in being able to cheat and break the law regardless of the consequences. This can be a way of life that is literally taught within the family and social milieu. If inculcated early enough, it can also give rise to certain personality traits that become an ingrained part of how the individual deals with those around him.

This may be learning how to carry out burglaries or other property crimes, or it may be the more subtle learning by example that occurs when a person is exposed to violence as a way of expressing anger within a dysfunctional family setting.

Criminal networks

It is important to recognize that most crimes are not the actions of lone individuals who are driven by some hidden force but are products of social interactions. Crimes are themselves part of a social process between an offender and an explicit or implicit victim, and often between offenders in the distribution and sale of illicit goods or services. The roots of criminality may therefore be found in criminals' styles of interacting with others and the networks of associates to which they belong.

Some Victorian reformers saw these social processes as like a form of contagion. The answer was therefore to separate offenders from each other. Quite elaborate prison designs were built to house this theory. They consisted of isolated cells in which each offender would be required to stay alone with only the Bible for company and no possibility of contact with other offenders, even in the chapel. This idea has left-over procedures in some prisons today, where being together with other prisoners, referred to as 'association', is often strictly controlled. 'Seclusion' is also used in many psychiatric facilities for similar reasons.

There can be little doubt that the experience of growing up in a community of criminals is a strong predictor of a person becoming criminal himself, although it is less clear exactly what it is about that experience which gives rise to criminality. Is it simply a matter of learning by example? Or does something more profound happen, changing the actual emotional and cognitive processes so that the person sees and feels the world differently? Or perhaps it is that a person's opportunities in life are limited and channelled because of their criminal associations – good schools and jobs may be denied them?

The idea that criminals are ordinary people trying to cope with difficult circumstances would take our hypothetical Dr Frankenstein in a quite different direction. Instead of trying to make a criminal person, he would have to create a criminal family, possibly within a criminal community. Many experts would want to take this a stage further and argue that it is a society in which there are large divisions between the rich and the poor that is the basis for criminality. From this perspective, offenders are merely making rational choices to try and survive in difficult circumstances with limited opportunities. This may not be a product of the whole society but relate to pockets of deprivation and alienation that may be the lot of poor immigrants or abused ethnic minorities, for example.

The problem with all these possibilities is that very many people grow up in a poor alienated community, or one dense with criminality, but manage to avoid being dragged into a life of crime. Some psychologists explain this by reference to 'protective factors', which may be supportive family or friends, a good teacher, their own intelligence, or special skills in sports, music, or mathematics, that give them a basis, framework, and opportunities that may not be available to their criminal associates. But all of this shows that the circumstances themselves are not a sole cause of criminality.

Varieties of criminality

Now it is time to admit that the task set for our hypothetical Dr Frankenstein was rather poorly defined. The request was to make a criminal without any consideration of what sort of criminal was required. Crime covers such a huge variety of activities that it is foolhardy to think there will be only one cause for all the forms that offending might take. Should we expect the same processes will give rise to a 12-year-old girl stealing a pretty headband from a department store in Paris, as will lead to a suicide bomber attempting to kill dozens of police recruits in Baghdad? Would the same genetics or psychology give rise to a young man setting fire to his estranged wife's car as to an armed robber stealing diamonds from a jewellery shop? Add the variation in laws across the world as to what is *defined* as criminal to this range of possibilities for what criminal actions are possible, and you have a very wide set of human activity that may be against the law.

In other words, any single explanation of criminality must assume that all crimes have something psychologically fundamental in common. It makes more sense to recognize that the many different forms of criminal action are likely to have many different causes. Furthermore, as the attentive reader will be starting to realize, it is extremely unlikely that any one process on its own can be blamed for a person committing criminal acts.

The range of actions that are criminal requires us to make some attempt to divide them up into subgroups so that we can consider the possible differences in causation. Such classification is, after all, the first step in any scientific endeavour. There would have been no theory of evolution without the clear identification of different species. Modern chemistry would not have got very far without the distinct identification of the elements and the periodic table. Unfortunately, classifying criminal actions is rather more difficult than classifying animals or chemical substances. The complexities emerge at a number of levels.

First, there is the problem, already hinted at, that legal definitions may not relate very closely to the psychological processes involved. If a burglar sets fire to a house he has broken into and in so doing kills the occupant, he may well be charged with murder. But should the crime be thought of as really arson or really burglary?

The second set of difficulties comes in classifying offenders who commit more than one crime. The rare man who kills his wife in a rage but has otherwise led a blameless life can be comfortably categorized as a murderer. But what if, as is more likely, he has previously been involved in robberies or fraud or arson? What subset of offenders do we assign him to? In various studies with offenders in prison, many of them will claim they are not 'real' criminals. They have a stereotype of what a criminal actually is, which may be a bank robber or street mugger. They will claim that defrauding their company, or forcing their sexual attentions on a woman, was an admittedly illegal misunderstanding, but not actually 'criminal'.

The resolution of the problems raised by the potential mix of illegal acts in a criminal's life is to explore which crimes tend to be committed by the same person; in other words, to examine the co-occurrence of crimes across many criminals. Although this will not give watertight compartments, it could give a general framework for considering different types of criminal. But it would only be of value if there really were clear differences between offenders in the broad types of crime they commit.

Many studies have explored this possibility, giving rise to a debate about whether offenders in general are 'specialists' or 'generalists'. The consensus is that many offenders, especially young offenders, are rather versatile in their criminal activity. The majority of people with any history of criminality will have carried out some form of theft and probably burglary at some point. But beyond this broad sweep of illegal activity, there does seem to be a tendency for some criminals to avoid violence and others to build up a dossier that is full of aggressive actions.

This brings us to the third difficulty in assigning offenders to neat subsets of criminal type: they change. A member of a juvenile gang of shoplifters may grow up into an aggressive rapist or a clever fraudster. This developmental process is often referred to as a 'criminal career', which should not be confused with a criminal who makes his living solely out of crime who may be called a 'career criminal'. However, it is rare for an offender to have a very distinct career progress as might be the case in a legitimate organization, starting off, for example, as an apprentice, moving up through middle management and on to being the 'big boss'. Such progressions do occur, especially within organized crime, as illustrated in quasi-fictional films such as *The Godfather*. But it is more often the case that a variety of opportunities and particular experiences make the offence trajectory less obvious.

For forensic psychologists, it is usually the offender who is the focus of interest, not the crime as such which may have brought the offender to the psychologist's office. So that when considering an offender, it will be important to explore all his offence history not just the most recent assault of which he might be convicted. This raises perhaps the most problematic aspect of determining which category of criminal the psychologist is dealing with. What do the mix of offences in the offender's criminal record have in common that will help the psychologist to make sense of the person she is trying to help?

This question requires detailed consideration of the nature of the criminal actions themselves. Is this a person who plans his crimes with a cool and calculating vengeance? Or is he an impulsive individual who just takes what he wants, whether it is a Rolex watch or sexual gratification? Such considerations require very close examination of exactly what happened in the crime and the context in which it occurred. It is out of such considerations that a psychological understanding of the individual offender will emerge.

Psychological explanations of violent crime

Given the huge spread of what counts as offending behaviour, it is perhaps not surprising that psychologists have tended to focus on the more bizarre and extreme forms of crime, especially those involving violence and sexual activity. For those criminals who commit such aggressive acts there is a plethora of psychological explanations and a growing number of intervention procedures. They draw on the ideas we reviewed earlier when considering crimes in general, relating to the interpretation, response, and consequences of the actions.

Most psychological explanations of aggressive crimes revolve around the proposal that some people just do not understand their interactions with others well enough, or have the social skills to manage those interactions. They have difficulty, as psychologists put it, in 'taking the role of the other': really understanding how others make sense of their world and react to the offender. As a consequence, they misinterpret what is happening and react with inappropriate violence. An extreme example of this is when a man thinks a woman is really consenting to sexual activity, when she is sure she is not. He may further believe that he has a right to sex, or become angry when thwarted. The only way he knows to deal with that anger is to lash out.

However, this is aggression that comes out of a heightened and uncontrolled emotionality. It is also often the case that a person may grow up in a milieu in which violence is an acceptable, or even encouraged, way of dealing with frustration or insult. This person can be thought to have learned to express himself violently. Such learning can go a stage further and be what is called 'instrumental': in other words, as opposed to the expression of anger or frustration the violence is a tool or instrument to control others and obtain what he wants. These are the calculating 'tough guys' who live their lives by inculcating fear of violence in others. They may be men who beat their wives to keep them under their thumb, or cold-blooded robbers who think nothing of attacking people in order to steal from them.

This process can give rise to a succession of violent actions, which is most apparent within relationships, often assigned the somewhat anodyne label of 'domestic violence', for there is nothing of the cosy 'domestic' quality to it. It is often thought to emerge from established, habitual patterns of interaction in which inherent conflicts within the relationship, often related to issues of power and control, escalate into violence.

In other cases, it may be that one member of the couple (often, but certainly not always, the man) has developed a violent way of dealing with frustration or jealousy. This can be presented, quite reasonably, from a feminist perspective as a product of how society at large, inappropriately, grants men the belief that they are ordained to be the dominant part of any relationship with a woman. Any threat to their view that they should have superior status is dealt with by attempts to coerce the woman back into the position the man deems she should occupy. Such coercion can often be very violent. The validity of this perspective finds support from consideration of how women were treated in many places in the past, and the very distressing information about how women are treated today in some countries.

Emotions and crime

Our explorations in how to make a criminal have, inevitably, sought to make use of processes outside of the control of the person, whether it be their biology, their psychological make-up, or their family and community. This reflects the stance of the social and biological sciences. They want their discipline to reveal what causes criminality. Society at large, and the courts in particular, see the matter quite differently. They put the blame for committing crime squarely on the shoulders of the offender. Consequently, there has been a growing movement amongst social scientists to try and determine what it is within the offender's experiences of committing crime that supports and maintains that activity. Putting it colloquially, 'what is it the offender gets out of illegal activity?'

It may be thought that the benefits to the criminal are obvious. Criminals want money, or control, or their actions are impulsive eruptions. Although in some cases this is certainly true, closer consideration indicates that often these objectives are not achieved, yet the offender continues to commit similar crimes over and over again. For example, often very little money is gained from a burglary or theft, especially when the percentage that is lost when trading illegal goods is taken into account. Violent assault may alienate more people than it brings under the offender's control. Aggressive acts that seem impulsive can be found to be repeated in similar situations so often that they can be predicted, thereby raising questions about how unplanned they really are.

The actual emotional experiences that are associated with criminal actions are often undervalued as explanations for criminality. Some offenders get real excitement from their thefts, frauds, or acts of violence. It is this emotional benefit which keeps them involved in a life of crime. Interviews with bank robbers, for instance, have revealed that they may seek out especially risky places to attack because of the thrill of getting away with the crime in those locations. Recent research has shown that even terrorists who are apparently driven by ideological goals are urged on by the exhilaration they feel from the devastation they plan to cause.

Criminal narratives

Some experts have taken this argument a stage further by proposing that many offenders assign roles to themselves and their victims within a view of their own personal life story, their 'inner narrative' – the story a person tells himself about himself. This will include his thoughts about his own capabilities and how others see him, but also some notion, however confused, of what he is trying to achieve with his crimes. He may see himself as a tragic figure striving against the forces of darkness, or as a victim suffering the vicissitudes of an enemy he cannot control. Many robbers and burglars see themselves as adventurers on a quest, or even professionals just doing a job.

The important point about these narratives is that they are constructed by the criminals themselves, however confused and incoherent their storylines may be. This implies that our Dr Frankenstein is on a fruitless task. It is the criminal himself who creates his offending, not some external force.

Conclusion

The hypothetical Dr Frankenstein is making two fundamental errors. One is that criminals are some distinct sub-species of human being and that it therefore makes sense to think of causes for criminality solely within the person. The other is the assumption that all criminals are alike. What has emerged in our review is the variety of criminality and the mix of biological, psychological, and social processes that underpin emerging self-concepts in offenders. These relate to their understanding of the world and the opportunities within it for legal and illegal activities.

The debate about the cause of criminal actions is often grossly oversimplified, into the attractively alliterative contrast between nature and nurture. Yet, neither the fundamental make-up of a person (their 'nature'), nor their upbringing and circumstances ('nurture'), are unitary phenomena. There are many aspects of a person that may combine to increase the risk of them offending, such as intellectual difficulties combining with physical difficulties, impulsive and aggressive tendencies. Or they may cancel each other out, as when a person who for one reason or another is aggressive but is also highly intelligent and very able to express himself is able to channel what could have been criminal into something that is seen as creative and iconoclastic.

There are also many different aspects of an environment that may be regarded as 'criminogenic'; mixing with other criminals may be more significant in a context of deprivation, for example, than when there are real opportunities for legitimate enterprise. But there may also be factors that protect against the possible influence of the surroundings, such as a caring, virtuous family that supports and disciplines its children.

Nor are nature and nurture distinctly separate from each other, either in their constituents or in how they combine to influence outcome. Children from disadvantaged backgrounds may be more open to physical trauma that can make it difficult for them to do well at school. This can lead to them being disruptive at school, possibly being excluded. This could then lead to them drifting into criminal activity as a way of finding some sense to their lives and some form of self-respect. But this may be aggravated or ameliorated by their inherent capabilities. Their families may or may not have the resources to find ways out of this destructive spiral or to provide later opportunities for gainful employment.

Individuals who may be born with a propensity to seek stimulation and a rather impulsive nature may have that channelled into sports and adventure holidays if they can find the resources to support these activities. Similarly, very capable people growing up in deprived contexts may turn their abilities to be effective at crime because that is the easiest option available. Even people who in some circumstances may be regarded as inherently 'psychopathic', because of their lack of emotion or remorse for harm they cause others, may become pillars of the community because they have the possibility of using their intelligence and network of contacts to succeed in business.

All this adds up to the realization that if we want to make a criminal, we cannot focus on just shaping a particular type of person. We have to create a criminal context for the individual to emerge within, which will include family and associates as well as a broader society and culture. As with any creative task, we would also have to be clear as to what sort of criminal we were trying to create. The process of making a murderer who led an innocent life until one day he killed his wife would be quite different from making a youngster who drifted into burglary from the age of ten and eventually killed a shopkeeper as part of a robbery, even though these two individuals may be sharing the same cell in prison. The difference between them will be most clearly revealed in what they think of themselves, the inner narrative that they have developed to give meaning and direction to their actions.

Chapter 3
Experts in court

Courtroom psychology

In August 1996, Daryl Atkins and William Jones robbed and shot
Eric Nesbitt. Jones testified that Atkins had pulled the trigger.
This being Virginia, USA, Atkins was sentenced to death.
A psychologist assessed Atkins and reported that he had an IQ of 59.
In response to an appeal, this was accepted by the Supreme Court as
indicating that Atkins was 'mentally retarded' ('learning-disabled'
would be a more acceptable term these days in the UK). The Court
ruled that it would be against the Eighth Amendment to the
American Constitution to execute a mentally retarded person
because such punishment would be 'cruel and unusual'.

This case illustrates the significant role that psychologists can play
on the basis of their assessment of the defendant, but also serves to
illustrate the ethical and professional challenges faced by any
psychologist giving evidence in court. Expert evidence is given to
assist the court in its decision, whether the expert agrees with that
decision or not.

What is an expert?

As in all legal matters, there is considerable debate about key
terms; in this situation, what 'expertise' means and what makes a

person acceptable to the courts as an 'expert'. Without reviewing the extensive case law on this matter and the large variations across jurisdictions, in essence an expert is someone who has some specialist knowledge or experience not otherwise available to the court. Experts are witnesses like any other who stand in court and give evidence. They have to take an oath and abide by court procedures, but their status as an 'expert' allows them to go beyond a statement of the facts as they know them. Other witnesses to the fact, such as eyewitnesses, or witnesses to good character, are only allowed to inform the court of what they actually know. Experts are allowed to go a stage further and offer an interpretation of the facts as they see them; in other words, to offer an opinion. This privileged position can give the expert somewhat more authority than someone who saw what happened. Yet it is potentially more subjective because it requires an exercise of judgement. This is why there are constraints on who is acceptable as an expert and on the sorts of opinion that can be offered.

The limits of expert evidence

Experts cannot offer opinions on any aspect relevant to the court proceedings; the opinion has to be within their area of competence and this is also constrained by legal limitations. One such limitation stems from what is known as 'the ultimate question', sometimes also known as 'the ultimate issue'. This is the question that the court itself must answer, which in a criminal case is usually whether the defendant is guilty or not. Other issues may come close to this, for instance whether the defendant or a key witness may be lying. But in all cases, the point is that the trial process is set up to answer a specific question and, although assistance may be given by experts in determining the answer, woe betide any expert who attempts to steal the thunder of the judge and jury.

One other area of legal proceedings that influences what psychological evidence can be offered is the need to avoid what is known as 'prejudicial information'. This is a barrier that few other legal experts have to deal with. Its workings can be illustrated in the following actual example. A man, let us call him Donald, was charged with the violent rape and murder of a woman in her own home. His defence was that he had consensual sex and then left the victim's house and that some other burglar must have later broken in and carried out the murder as part of the burglary. To support his case, he wanted to bring forward evidence from a psychologist that such a violent assault was completely out of character.

The psychologist could determine that the man exhibited no fantasies or other personality traits that would be consistent with such aggression. Furthermore, he was known locally as some sort of 'stud' with whom women he met at night clubs would happily have sex. In interview with the psychologist, he admitted to picking up as many as three or four women a week in this way. In addition, his criminal background only included theft and fraud. There was no history of violence at all. The psychologist could therefore build up a pattern of the consistencies in the defendant's background that would support his claim to be of non-violent character.

However, such evidence was not allowed by the court. The view was that if the jury knew that Donald a) led a promiscuous sex life and b) had committed any sort of crimes in the past, that this would colour their view of him. They would be prejudiced against him and therefore not consider the facts of the case carefully enough. In rare cases where the values in favour of the defendant would strongly outweigh the prejudicial implications, such evidence may be allowed.

Therefore the role of the forensic psychologist in court is to give advice that will help the jury come to their own decisions. Or in the case of family courts and other legal situations in which only professionals are making the judgements, the expert is allowed to offer opinions that are based directly on their particular expertise, but they must not stray into comments on the facts or the ultimate decision that the court must make.

However, there are circumstances in which the forensic psychologist will not be under these legal constraints. Lawyers may seek guidance from psychologists to help them prepare a case, throwing light on the defendant or issues of testimony, even an appropriate way to cross-examine a witness. An illustration of this is the case in which a crucial issue was whether the defendant was left-handed or not. A psychologist who had studied left-handedness was able to point out that it was not a simple all-or-nothing preference; people could prefer to use their right foot when kicking a ball and have a dominant right eye but be left-handed. This gave the attorney the opportunity of opening up the question in court of whether being left-handed was as crucial or clear-cut as was being claimed. He was able to ask questions about preferences for kicking and other behavioural details, without the need for any expert testimony.

Forensic psychology expertise is also less constrained when the proceedings, although operating in a legal framework, are not a formal court process in which the expert is giving evidence under oath, such as in employment tribunals, probation hearings, or risk assessments in the context of health care. There are also a number of other forms of consultancy that forensic psychologists may give to assist lawyers which relate to aspects of the legal process rather than the defendant or witnesses, such as how juries make decisions. What this all illustrates is that the role of forensic psychologists depends considerably on the particular jurisdiction and legal context in which they are operating and the legal questions they are asked to answer.

The significance of the legal context

A crucial difference in legal context on the way forensic experts are dealt with is whether the legal process is broadly what is known as

6. An expert giving evidence in court

'adversarial' compared with being 'magisterial' (or 'inquisitorial', as it is often called). The former, more characteristic of English-speaking nations, has a distinct prosecution and defence that are played out in an open court in front of a jury, which is typically a random selection of members of the public who live locally. The crucial point about a jury, and thus a major distinction between the two systems, is that they are deliberately chosen because they do not have any special knowledge, understanding, or experience of the law. By contrast, the 'magisterial' system is one in which one or more professional judges (magistrates) make all the decisions. Sometimes this is done mainly on the basis of documents presented to them without the extensive courtroom debates that Hollywood, based in the US adversarial system, is so fond of. Furthermore, in many jurisdictions the magistrates also oversee the actual investigation of the crime.

In an adversarial system, experts are typically called in by either the prosecution or the defence (although they are formally supposed to be merely giving guidance to the court). They are technically giving their evidence to the jury, and so to some degree are constrained to make it as non-technical as possible, especially given the cut and thrust of cross-examination by lawyers acting for the 'other side'. When the case is fought in front of a jury of ordinary folk, the legal systems tend to believe that members of the public can be unfairly persuaded by a plausible 'expert' and so must be protected from anything the expert may say that would be too directly influential. In a magisterial context, experts are given more rein to offer direct opinions on the central issues of the case. The belief is that if expert opinion is offered to the professionals who are making the decisions, rather than a jury of laypeople, they can accept it or ignore it at will.

In the British and many other legal systems that are dominated by the adversarial framework, there are nonetheless many courts that are essentially magisterial, in which decisions are usually made by judges, professional lawyers, or people specifically appointed and trained to be magistrates, rather than a randomly selected jury. This includes the higher courts of appeal, which deal with challenges to the decisions of the lower courts, and also various high-level legal enquiries often known as 'judicial reviews'.

Other processes, notably coroners' courts, which have the duty of determining the cause of death, and family courts, which often deal with matters concerning the custody of children and parental access to them, are typically handled by one or more trained lawyers acting as judges, rather than a jury. A variety of courts dealing with civil matters such as contested wills or financial claims also are usually magisterial. Other procedures that are governed by the law but that do not include a formal criminal or civil court overseen by trained lawyers or judges also tend to be magisterial. These include, for example, employment tribunals which deal with unfair dismissal, or even parole boards determining whether a prisoner should be allowed out of prison prior to the end of his sentence. In all of these proceedings, forensic psychologists may offer expert opinions.

One step even further removed from the full ritual of court proceedings than tribunals and parole boards are meetings of professionals to discuss particular cases. These may be to assess the risk of individuals harming themselves or others, or their ability to be effective parents. In these proceedings, the psychologist contributes an assessment of the key individuals, usually as an integral part of the team. They will be part of the debate with none of the formalities of presenting evidence and being cross-examined as in a court of law.

In the proceedings without a jury, forensic psychologists can have a much more significant role because they are advising the magistrates and decision-makers directly about crucial aspects of the case in front of them. The psychologist will be open to challenge, and there will often be the equivalent of a 'prosecution' and a 'defence' trying to support or undermine the points the expert is offering, but matters that could be prejudicial, in the legal sense mentioned above, and even dealing with the ultimate question, may be open to an expert if there is no jury present. As mentioned, but worth repeating because of its significance, the decision-makers in such cases are ready to ignore those opinions, if they deem them unfounded, in a way that it is assumed a lay jury would not.

The basis of forensic psychology evidence

Experts have to offer the courts or similar proceedings evidence that would not be available by any other means. What are the bases for such evidence? An understanding of the psychological explanations of crime is only a very small first step towards providing some useful evidence. It is the scientific methods that are the foundations of modern psychology which provide the most useful tools from which to derive evidence.

One of the best informed and most interesting early reviews of how psychology can contribute to the law came from the late

Professor Lionel Haward. He was a tall, balding, bespectacled, neatly dressed clinical psychologist, with a dry but rich sense of humour, which was sometimes rather risqué. He looked every inch the stereotype of the expert witness, but behind this urbane countenance was a profound, pioneering approach to how psychologists should contribute to court proceedings. In one of the first major books reviewing forensic psychologists' actual contributions to the legal process, drawing on his own extensive experience in the witness box, Haward pointed out that there are a number of different roles that psychologists can play in legal proceedings.

The clinical role

A major foundation he calls 'clinical'. This is based on the experience that psychologists have of working with patients (or 'clients') in some form of therapeutic setting. This is normally helping people with mental illness or mental disorder, giving the psychologist experience in many aspects of mental abnormality as well as interviewing skills that lawyers may not have. Haward provides an example of this from his casebook. A woman was accused of stealing a silver trophy; however, another person who worked with her came forward and confessed to the theft. In interview with this second person, as part of his defence, Haward explored the significance of the trophy to him, using psychological procedures that would be relevant in a clinical interview for therapeutic purposes. During the course of this, the man revealed his fondness for the accused woman and his desire to protect her from a conviction that would ruin her life, eventually admitting that he was not guilty of the crime to which he had confessed.

A more common illustration would be one in which a client is claiming compensation for some accident and asks the psychologist to give evidence for the debilitating effect of that accident, especially the impact on the client's mental state. This can be very difficult for the psychologist because the client's outstanding compensation claim could itself have an influence on his mental state, causing anxiety or a reluctance to get on with his life for fear of downgrading his claim. In these situations, an experienced clinician would draw upon similar previous cases he was aware of as well as careful interview strategies, special psychological tests, and a review of relevant published work he could find, in order to provide as objective a report as possible.

Assessment

In many contexts, but most notably when assessing a client, psychologists use what are generally known as 'psychometric procedures', or more generally 'psychological tests'. Atkins's IQ was assessed using the most widespread form of psychological assessment, an 'intelligence test'. Such measuring instruments as intelligence tests are in common use across psychology. But there are legions of others that can be of value to legal proceedings. These include assessment of many forms of intellectual ability, educational attainment, or cognitive skills, some specifically established to diagnose brain diseases such as those associated with Alzheimer's. They may also cover measures of various aspects of personality – whether it be styles of interpersonal interaction, extroversion, or ways of coping with stress.

Several of these procedures use what are known as 'projective' techniques that have their origins in Freudian ideas of the unconscious. They consist of ambiguous images that the client has to interpret. The best known of these is the Rorschach inkblot test. A standard set of symmetrical smudges, initially produced by folding an inkblot into a piece of paper, are presented, and the respondent has to describe what he or she sees in the vague image. This technique had its origins in the parlour game of 'Blotto' that was very popular a hundred years ago. The game was to give a meaning to the indeterminate image. Another commonly used procedure is the Thematic Apperception Test (TAT), in which the patient is shown an ambiguous picture, say of a young man sitting on a bed with a woman sitting on the other side of the bed

Examples of psychological assessment procedures relevant to the forensic context

Personality assessment

Projective:

Rorschach inkblot test

Thematic Apperception Test (TAT)

Szondi test (a curious test not used much these days)

Objective:

Minnesota Multiphasic Personality Inventory (MMPI), 2nd edition

Million Clinical Mulitaxial Inventory (MCMI), 3rd edition

Personality Assessment Inventory (PAI)

Intellect/cognition

Wechsler Adult Intelligence Scale (WAIS), 4th edition

Trail Making Tests A and B

Luria-Nebraska Neurophysiological Battery

Specific forensic assessments

Structured professional judgement:

Sexual Violence Risk - 20 (SVR-20)

Psychopathy Check List - Revised (PCL-R)

Historical Clinical Risk Management - 20 (HCR-20)

Juvenile Sex Offender Assessment Protocol (J-SOAP)

Risk for Sexual Violence Protocol (RSVP)

Actuarial risk assessment:

Static-2002 / Static-99 (offender's history as indicators of risk)

Violence Risk Appraisal Guide (VRAG)

Malingering:

Structured Interview of Reported Symptoms (SIRS)

Test of Memory Malingering (TOMM)

with her back to him. The task is to tell a story that the picture illustrates.

In all projective techniques, the idea is that the respondent will reveal something about their unconscious or hidden motives and thoughts through the way they interpret the images. Detailed scoring procedures have been devised, often now computer-based, for analysing responses. A simplified example would be that someone describing sex and violence in the images would be thought to be revealing the significance of this in their lives. By contrast, a person building an interpretation around future aspirations would be assumed to have a more mature and forward-looking approach to life.

In addition, there are many assessment tools that have been specifically developed for use with offenders. Most commonly, these cover assessments of the risk that the individual will commit another crime, or a violent crime, in the near or distant future. Tests have been developed for a wide range of other criminal issues as well. These include tests that explore the sexual preferences of an individual, or an offender's competency to understand the trial process. Most notably, there are checklists that assess a person's level of psychopathy. This latter does not require the respondent to fill in a questionnaire (for the obvious reason that a psychopath would be expected to lie); instead, the person is interviewed and those who have had contact with him are also questioned, so that a number of pointers can be indicated on the psychopathy checklist.

Standardization of psychological tests

What all these measuring instruments have in common is that they are developed using established psychometric procedures, often known as 'standardizing' a test. Without going into the detailed technicalities here, in essence the psychometric process consists of getting the test completed initially by many people – often hundreds of people, sometimes thousands. Their responses are then analysed in relation to each other and to other external criteria. The classical illustration of this is the development of IQ tests. The number of correct answers given by children of each age is calculated so that any given child can be compared with others of the same age. To make a child's score on the test easily interpretable, the average score for each age group is set at 100, so that a score of 59, as in Atkins's case, can be seen as far below average. The statistics actually allow the precise calculation that fewer than 1 in 100 of the population would have an IQ of 59 or below.

The population distribution of scores achieved on a test are called the 'norms' for a test. It is the process of comparing an individual's scores with these norms which makes these measuring instruments different from the sorts of questionnaires that may be found in magazines. In those questionnaires, arbitrary score values are created by journalists and given interpretations. They also distinguish them from public opinion polls in which the interest is solely in the proportion of a given population who agree with a specified opinion, such as who would be the best prime minister.

Beyond the ability to weigh the scores any individual obtains against a comparable population, the development of tests also seeks to relate the scores to other issues external to the test. For instance, an IQ test would not even be of academic interest if the scores people obtained on it did not relate reasonably closely to a person's actual educational achievements, or abilities other than taking tests. To take another even more extreme example, if serial criminals did not on average have higher psychopathy scores than those who led a blameless life, then the measure of psychopathy could not be taken very seriously. This relationship to external indicators is usually referred to as the 'validity' of a test.

Psychological tests vary enormously in the thoroughness and appropriateness of their norms and how well their validity has been established. In particular, their norms may not be appropriate in places different from where the test was originally developed; an indicator of psychopathy developed in the USA may have little value in countries with very different cultures, such as India, Nigeria, or Russia. Until the test has been translated and standardized in those different contexts, its use may be counterproductive. Also, measuring instruments that look as if they are of great relevance to criminality may turn out to be quite invalid. An interesting illustration of this is that it may be assumed that lack of sophistication in moral reasoning is the hallmark of a criminal, but until this has been proven it is merely an hypothesis.

However, despite many criticisms of psychometric measuring instruments, they do provide the backbone to a lot of expert opinion. This is not least because the courts are more comfortable with a view that is based on a standard procedure that many professionals agree is appropriate. Tests also provide a standardized framework for describing a person, thus making it much easier to prepare a report than searching afresh for relevant and appropriate terms.

The most widely used psychological test in the forensic context, especially in the USA, is the Minnesota Multiphasic Personality Inventory (MMPI). This comes in a number of versions, but the standard form consists of 567 questions and takes between an hour and an hour and a half to complete. The questions consist of statements such as:

> My daily life is full of things that keep me engrossed.
> There often seems to be a lump in my throat.
> I enjoy detective stories.
> Once in a while I think of things too bad to speak about.
> My sex life is pleasing.

The respondents then have to say whether the statements are true or false with regard to themselves. A complex and highly developed scoring system is then applied to the answers in order to indicate a wider range of potential problems in the individual, including schizophrenia, hypochondriasis, depression, and the sort of psychopathy that relates to disrespect for society's rules. The test also includes measures of whether the respondent is faking good or faking bad, or generally lying, but as with all attempts to tell how honest respondents are being, there is considerable debate about how valid they are. The very extensiveness and detail of the MMPI is probably one reason why there has been such a vast range of studies using it despite continuing discussion of its utility.

Challenges to the scientific value of psychometric instruments are much more vocal for projective techniques. The problems here are manifold. If the test is measuring unconscious aspects of the individuals that they may not even be aware of themselves, what will be suitable external criteria against which to test the test? The issues that the tester claims are being revealed may never become manifest because, after all, they are unconscious.

Even more challenging is the determination of what is characteristic of the response. This relates to the general issue known in psychometrics as 'reliability'. That is, the likelihood that carrying out the same test under very similar conditions on more than one occasion will give the same results. When the response given has a very open-ended quality, such as telling a TAT story or interpreting an inkblot, there is a very real possibility that different testers (or the same tester on different occasions) will identify different aspects of the comments. For example, when a person comments on an inkblot, should the tester note the part of the inkblot that is mentioned, whether the respondent implies movement or colour in the meaning given, or just focus on the content of the meaning? In all these cases, what population or sample should the responses be compared with to determine how unusual they are?

Despite these problems, the Rorschach inkblot test is still very popular and used widely to give court assessments. This is in part because a procedure developed by the American psychologist John E. Exner claims to overcome these challenges by providing a very precise process for interpreting responses that is supported by computing technology. A major weakness in this more precise approach, though, is that not every tester follows it, and the courts may be ignorant of the consequences of such negligence on the part of the tester. It may be for these reasons that the validity of the Rorschach test is still widely challenged, even if some people claim it can even help to detect cancer in its respondents.

The experimental role

A somewhat different role to which Haward draws attention is one in which the skills in carrying out an experiment are used to test whether claims that the evidence on offer is likely to be true. One such example on which the present author gave evidence related to the claim from a defendant that he had never made the confession which a police officer insisted was the verbatim transcript of an interview held with the defendant. This was before police interviews were recorded, and indeed the case was part of an accumulation of reasons why, in the UK at least, virtually all interviews with suspects are recorded these days.

As was common police practice, the times of the start and end of the interview were recorded in the police log book. There was thus a simple question of whether a police officer really could write all that he claimed he had written in the time available. A simple experiment was therefore set up, inspired by many that Haward carried out. A student known to write very quickly was given the task of writing down the alleged verbatim statement when read to her at a reasonable talking pace by another person. It was found that it was only just possible under these conditions for the student to complete the task in the time available. There are established writing speeds for dictation, and when compared to these our student was indeed found to be at the upper limit of what are known capabilities. Evidence was consequently given that the police officer in question would have had to be a remarkably proficient transcriber to have written the interview in the time claimed and that it was therefore just possible he had done so, but rather unlikely, especially when the time taken for asking questions and pauses before answering were taken into account.

This sort of experimental study often relates to challenges to statements from key witnesses. Probably the most memorable of Haward's experiments in this context harked back to Munsterberg's defence of the Flemish weavers. He was called in to help defend a local mayor who had been accused of indecent exposure in a public toilet. This resulted from two police officers following up complaints of indecent activities by hiding themselves in a cubicle in the public conveniences, peering through a grill in the door.

The defendant claimed that he had been wearing a pink scarf at the time and that the enthusiastic police officers, being keen to make an arrest, had been so primed to expect indecency that they had misinterpreted this innocent apparel for a part of his anatomy. Haward tested this by setting up an experiment in which naïve subjects were shown photographs, under limited lighting conditions, of the mayor wearing his scarf. They were given the expectation that something untoward was illustrated in the pictures and asked to indicate when they saw it and what it was. He found that one picture in every eight was believed to represent an indecent act. Haward offered these results together with an explanation of the psychological processes involved and citation of other studies illustrating the power of expectancies on the interpretation of ambiguous images. The attorney used this report as the basis for challenging the police evidence. The mayor was acquitted.

The actuarial role

In both the clinical and experimental roles, the psychologist will often draw upon known statistical relationships to support his case. So the role that draws on the probabilities of certain indicators is not quite as distinct as the other two. However, it is useful to identify because it shows the developing power of forensic psychology as a scientific discipline. It is similar to DNA and fingerprint evidence in which the probability of the sample being from a given individual supports the case before the court.

It should be noted that with fingerprints, and to a lesser extent DNA, evidence of identity is far from foolproof. There are important cases in which fingerprint experts have claimed the fingerprints to be those of the suspect only for it to be shown beyond any doubt that the suspect was innocent. Actuarial calculations are always open to question. They are best treated as informed bets on which the court may be willing to put its shirt, or, in the legal formulation, put the decision 'beyond reasonable doubt'. It is worth noting here that in civil courts where the decision relates to relationships between individuals, the legal test is weaker. The decision has to be on the balance of probabilities. This thus gives estimates of probability rather more weight.

There have been attempts to use psychological evidence to determine the identity of the perpetrator. This notably takes the form of claiming that the 'profile' of the perpetrator revealed through the details of the crime fits the accused; or in some cases attempting to use as a defence the claim that the actions in the offence indicate a personality that is totally different to the accused. Fortunately, such attempts have eventually failed on appeal, even if the court initially accepted them. The statistics are just not precise or strong enough to be used in such a powerful way. There may be some general indication, for example that a person who commits a murder is likely to be known to be violent, but there are far too many murderers who have no history of violence and violent people who never murder to provide convincing probabilities. Even when much more precise details of the actions in a crime are considered, the information relating them to particular offender characteristics is not robust enough to be used in a court of law.

In reality, any 'profiling' evidence runs the risk of having the psychologist answer the ultimate question. By saying the accused does or does not match to characteristics that would be uniquely expected of the offender is tantamount to claiming that he is guilty or innocent. The courts are thus understandably reluctant to accept any expertise that could be construed as 'offender profiling'.

Conclusions

The role that forensic psychologists play in court proceedings depends considerably on the particular jurisdiction to which they are contributing. As they have developed ever more systematic, and apparently objective, procedures on which to base their expert opinions, they have found their way into an ever wider range of legal activities. Some of these contributions take a standard format that has become routine. Others are specifically fashioned to deal with the issues in a particular case. All of these, though, utilize theories, methods, principles, and procedures that are unique to forensic psychologists and their clinical experiences. This is opening up an even broader range of involvement in legal procedures, as we shall see in the next chapter.

Chapter 4
Psychology and legal proceedings

Insanity in court

One of the major contributions of psychologists to legal proceedings is in assessing whether defendants at the time of the crime were unable either to understand the nature of what they were doing or, if they did understand, to recognize that it was wrong. This is different from not knowing it was illegal, because, as is often quoted, 'ignorance is no defence before the law'. Rather it is a lack of moral awareness of the wrongful nature of the action. It is this subtlety that often confuses lay discussions of obviously heinous crimes such as the serial killing of strangers. The killings may appear to be so beyond what is morally acceptable that the murderer by any reasonable standards must be regarded as mad. However, if he has enough contact with reality to be aware of what he is doing, and that it is wrong, then under the law he cannot plead insanity. This is why very few serial killers are ever found not guilty by reason of insanity.

The differences between legal and public understanding of insanity often stir debate. A man who carries out actions that are difficult to comprehend, such as killing his children as revenge against his wife, or killing complete strangers eating in a McDonald's, may be regarded by many people as 'out of his mind'.

For the courts, though, if he knows what he is doing and that it is wrong, he is sane.

The insanity defence has implications for dealing with children because most jurisdictions accept that children below a certain age cannot be considered able to tell right from wrong. Interestingly, this minimum age of criminal liability varies from 7 years old in India to 18 in Brazil, being 10 for England and Wales and for federal crimes in the USA. But in order to allow children to give evidence, a psychologist may also be called in to establish that the young witness really does know the difference between right and wrong, and truth and lies.

A particularly difficult assessment to make can be in cases where the defendant claims some form of temporary insanity that may be expressed as an irresistible impulse. This has a number of subtleties. If the action was one in which the person had lost contact with reality, possibly hallucinating, then he may be found not guilty by reason of insanity. A more extreme form of this could be what is known as 'automatism', in which the person was totally unaware of his actions, possibly because he was asleep at the time. Such a person would be acquitted because he had no *mens rea*.

These issues are all part of general claims that the defendant had reduced legal liability because of some form of mental illness. If this illness is characteristic of the defendant, then the psychologist's task is to assess its prevalence across the defendant's life history and any role it may have played in the offence with which he is charged. There are established psychological tests that can be drawn on to help form such a judgement, but the current professional view is that at best these can be helpful as part of a broader clinical interview, but are unlikely to be sufficiently valid to be used on their own.

An assessment that can relate to an insanity plea but which is rather different is to determine if a person is competent to stand trial. Competency to stand trial is the individual's general ability to be able to make appropriate decisions and understand what is happening in court. The crucial difference from insanity assessment is that competency relates to mental capacity at various stages in the legal process, whereas an insanity plea focuses on the mental state at the time of the crime.

One clear example of a competency assessment is the case of Theon Jackson, a 27-year-old deaf mute arrested for stealing. He was found to have a very low IQ and was also unable to communicate effectively enough to participate in his own defence. This led to a ruling that he was unfit to stand trial and thus either had to be released or committed to some form of managed institution.

There are a number of standardized tests for measuring competency, but the issue is so closely intertwined with actual legal processes it is rare for these to be relied upon for evidence. Most professionals prefer to carry out in-depth interviews and utilize more general measures of mental illness and intellectual ability. This allows them to determine whether the defendant really is able to understand the legal process he is part of and to communicate effectively with his legal team. If the forensic psychologist can go a stage further and draw on her understanding of what may be causing any deficits, then this will strengthen any case she can put before the court in support of or against fitness to stand trial. As part of this process, an assessment of whether the defendant is malingering would be a crucial component. Some psychological tests directly aim to reveal attempts to feign mental illness or other forms of incompetency.

Broadening contributions

The different roles that psychologists take in legal proceedings have opened up a range of topics that now go beyond the considerations of mental illness and fitness to plead. This broadening variety of contributions draws on clinical experience as well as many different studies, sometimes carried out in relation to particular cases but more often as general background research that eventually finds its way into the legal process. Consideration of some of these wider areas of expert evidence reveals just how deeply psychologists are becoming embedded in jurisprudence.

False confessions

One area that is particularly intriguing is the situation in which a person may falsely confess to a crime. It often surprises people, even experienced police officers, that someone will confess to a crime that they know they did not commit. Yet from the earliest psychological considerations of evidence, it has been known that false confessions occur often enough to be a source of real concern for the police and the courts. One dramatic historical illustration of this is that when Charles Lindbergh's son was kidnapped in 1932, nearly 200 people confessed to the crime. Similarly, more than 100 people confessed to the murder in 1986 of Swedish Prime Minister Olaf Palme.

There are many reasons why people may falsely confess, the most obvious relating to a desire to protect another person or to escape from the coercion in an interrogation, or indeed torture, with some idea of being released once having confessed. However, a small number develop the belief that they have indeed committed the crime.

To understand how an innocent person can convince himself that he has committed a crime, the malleability of memory needs to be appreciated. Many years of psychological research have shown that memory is not like an old-fashioned photographic plate that fades with time. Rather, it is constructed on the basis of knowledge of possibilities and patterns from fragments of what was noticed at the time. There is now a very large body of research that shows how this process can be influenced by events that happen subsequent to what is being remembered. A particularly potent influence can be questions that are asked about the key incident. If these questions imply things that did not happen, then in later recall the person may have internalized these suggestions and now believe he has remembered them. For example, if a person is asked about a red car that passed during the events that were witnessed, even though there never was a red car, then it is possible that in later interviews the person may genuinely think they remember a red car passing.

In situations in which a person has no memory at all of what happened, perhaps because of drink or drugs, they may be even more vulnerable to suggestions of their guilt. Some people may even feel remorse for what has happened, even though they were not involved, and confess because they think they ought to be guilty.

However, there is a subgroup of people who come into police custody who are especially vulnerable to the even implicit pressures that may be present in the interview process. Some of these people may be suffering from a mental illness, such as schizophrenia, that makes it difficult for them to distinguish fantasy from reality, or they may be intellectually impaired and not really aware of what they are admitting to. Indeed, there are indications that in some cultures it is expected that a person from a lowly background will agree with whatever a person in authority proposes. So if told they are guilty, they will accept this without question. Forensic psychologists will be in a position to explore these possibilities and to advise the courts and other professionals whether the person has such propensities that make them likely to falsely confess.

Gudjonsson and others, who have studied proneness to suggestibility, claim that there are also other less obvious characteristics of some people that make them particularly susceptible to influence. To test for this, Gudjonsson developed a procedure to measure just how predisposed to be suggestible a person is. He has used this test in many courts of law around the world to support defendants' claims that they falsely confessed due to their susceptibility to the interrogation process. Most notably, he gave evidence for the Birmingham Six, all of whom were eventually released, although originally convicted of planting in pubs bombs that killed 21 people. He found that the four of the six who falsely confessed to leaving the bombs had much higher scores on his measure of suggestibility than the two who did not confess.

Gudjonsson's examination consists of reading a narrative to the person being tested, who is then asked to say what he remembers about the story. Subsequently, he is questioned closely about the story. Some of these questions imply aspects to the story that were not present in it and the respondent is told they have made some important errors so must answer the questions again. It is the degree to which the person being examined then alters his answers and the way in which he alters them that is used to indicate how suggestible he is to severe questioning. Gudjonsson's procedure is not without serious critics, but the readiness with which law courts have accepted it does illustrate a willingness to include psychological assessments if they have a good enough pedigree.

Recovered memories

It is claimed that sometimes, as part of therapy, a patient may come to remember traumas from their earlier years that they had forgotten. These 'recovered memories' are often of some form of abuse. Such declarations of having been abused have then been used as evidence in court to get convictions against the alleged culprit. There are many cases in which this has resulted in a blameless person, often a father or other close relative, being imprisoned for many years. The problem is determining whether the memory is recovered or has been falsely, and perhaps innocently, encouraged in the mind of the patient.

It is difficult for judges and juries to believe that someone would falsely, but honestly, remember a significant event if it had never occurred. But the ability of some people to have very clear memories of events that seem even more unlikely than being abused as a child, such as alien abduction, shows just how careful the courts must be. If there is no corroborating evidence, how can it be decided if the memory is accurate or not? Normal criteria such as the vividness of the memory and the confidence the person has in recounting it may not be appropriate if the report has been developed over many months in sessions led by a therapist who is convinced that the patient's symptoms are the product of abuse.

Part of the foundation of modern psychoanalysis was Sigmund Freud's consideration of why his patients claimed they had been abused as children when that was apparently not the case. Freud saw this as an expression of a patient's unconscious desires that were part of the psychological problem that had brought them to him. In other words, Freud claimed the patient's problems were not the result of abuse. By contrast, therapists operating within a tradition that has a direct descent from Freud's believe that traumatic events the patient cannot recall did occur and can be brought into the light through the appropriate therapeutic processes. The challenge to memories 'recovered' in this way is that the claim that they are genuine ignores the malleability of human memory, which we have noted in relation to false confessions and other aspects of witness statements.

Syndrome evidence

Complex psychological phenomena and the analysis of them are difficult for the courts to digest. This is partly because judges believe they know a lot about human beings and that juries should be allowed to draw on their own experiences to make sense of what they are told. If a standardized test can be used to support a psychological conclusion, then this does add an extra level of expertise beyond that available to the court from personal experience. Similarly, if the behavioural issues being explored can be presented as analogous to some form of medical diagnosis, it may also be more acceptable than mere 'professional opinion'. It is in this context that a burgeoning number of psychological 'syndromes' have found their way into legal proceedings. However, it is important to say right away that neither lawyers nor many psychologists are comfortable with this medicalization of patterns of behaviour, but this has not stopped such syndromes becoming part of the vocabulary of forensic psychology.

Post-traumatic stress disorder (PTSD)

By far the most common psychological syndrome to be used in evidence is post-traumatic stress disorder (PTSD). This has a long and chequered history, being part of 'shell-shock' recognized during the First World War, or what was called 'battle fatigue' during the Second World War. There was even a phenomenon identified in the American Civil War that was called 'soldier's heart'. Initially, all these extreme reactions to the experience of battle were dismissed as cowardice or a weak personality. There were cases in the First World War of soldiers being shot for cowardice or desertion who would now be recognized as suffering from PTSD. The clinical understanding of the effects of severe trauma has helped to produce a more enlightened understanding of what people experience in the heat of war, and this has also provided a framework for evaluating the psychological impact of many other traumatic situations.

Some estimates suggest that as many as one in ten of the population suffer PTSD during their lives. An illustration would be if you were involved in a driving accident and were consequently reluctant to drive or overly cautious when on the road, responding with a sudden surge of anxiety whenever you became aware of squealing tyres, then you would have the basis of at least a mild form of PTSD. If these symptoms lasted for two or three weeks, it would probably be labelled 'acute stress disorder'.

Unlike other forms of mental disorder, PTSD does require a clear cause, a traumatic event that can be regarded as beyond normal human experience, involving intense fear, helplessness, or horror. For the diagnosis to be assigned, the psychological consequences of this trauma must be shown to have lasted for longer than a month and to include upsetting memories, flashbacks, distressing dreams, or some mixture of these. In addition, the person must feel the need to avoid anything associated with the trauma, such as places or people, or even some of the memories. The fourth component of the disorder is an increased sensitivity to potential threats, especially from anything linked to the cause of the trauma, with associated anxiety and anguish, often indicated through sleep disturbance. If some aspects of each of these four constituents are present, then PTSD is diagnosed. The number, intensity, and longevity of the symptoms are drawn on to indicate the severity of the disorder.

PTSD has been accepted in US courts as a form of mental illness and thus used as mitigating circumstances for a violent attack. In one case, the New Jersey Superior Court accepted that a violent attack by an ex-soldier, on a police officer, was a product of a flashback in which the police officer was mistaken for an enemy combatant. This use of PTSD as part of an insanity plea has been taken even further in a Canadian court decision in a case of a sexual assault of a child. The defendant claimed he had PTSD as the result of an incident that had occurred whilst he was on a peacekeeping mission in Bosnia. He had interrupted a sexual assault on a child by killing the attacker. He argued in court that the assault of which he was accused was the result of a re-enactment of that event. The judge accepted that he was insane at the time of the crime, being unable to appreciate the nature of what he was doing. Needless to say, many experts are concerned about this extension of PTSD as an insanity defence in crimes of intimate violence. The extent of black-outs and memory loss as part of PTSD, as in so many other areas of memory, are extremely difficult to validate.

The main use of PTSD is in accident claims where it provides a well-tried and clear set of criteria for assessing the psychological impact of the accident. However, even this apparently obvious application is open to question. There is considerable evidence that the impact of any trauma depends on the psychological wellbeing of the person before the event occurs. Also experiences after the trauma, such as social support or loss of employment, can have an impact on the development of PTSD. Most problematic is the clear indication that PTSD may be more long-lasting and severe if there is ongoing litigation in which it could play a role.

Battered woman syndrome

Another syndrome that found its way into court, possibly even before PTSD, was battered woman syndrome (BWS). This has been used by attorneys to explain why a woman who has suffered extensive physical abuse over a period of time would still fail to leave the relationship, even when the batterer was absent or asleep. The characteristics of the syndrome revolve around the idea that the victim is actually taught by the offender to become helpless. 'Learned helplessness' is a phenomenon first observed in animals that were unable to escape from electric shocks in experiments. They eventually stopped trying to avoid the shocks and just lay there listlessly. This passivity in relation to unavoidable, random abuse has since been found in many individuals.

When the random abuse is part of a relationship between human beings, there is a mix of psychological processes that underlie the helplessness. This includes the victim believing the abuse is her fault and that there may be something she can do to stop it happening in the future, or more direct fear for her life or her children. The abuse will often have psychological blackmail components too, such as telling the victim her children will be taken from her if she reports the violence. All of this is often supported by an irrational belief that the perpetrator is all-powerful and all-knowing.

Some psychological syndromes that have been used as evidence in court

Battered child syndrome (BCS)
Battered woman syndrome (BWS)
Child sexual abuse syndrome (CSAS)
Child sexual abuse accommodation syndrome (CSAAS)
False memory syndrome (FMS)
Munchausen syndrome by proxy (MSP), also called factitious disorder by proxy
Parental alienation syndrome (PAS)
Post-traumatic stress disorder (PTSD)
Rape trauma syndrome (RTS)
Recovered memory syndrome (RMS)
Traumatic brain injury (TBI)

Explaining female actions

What is notable about many syndromes accepted by the courts is that they relate directly to women's actions, rather than men's, often explaining the actions of female victims when they do not accord with popular, stereotypical views of how women would be expected to act. Battered women, as we have noted, may not run away or fight back, and the BWS can help juries to understand why that is. A number of other similar syndromes have also been accepted as explanations for apparently surprising behaviour by women, or as evidence of diminished responsibility or mitigating circumstances. They therefore generate lively debate as to whether they are forms of misogyny in disguise and not really established conditions like those of a medical nature.

Premenstrual stress syndrome, in which women at a particular stage of the menstrual cycle may be more emotionally vulnerable and suffer a mixture of physical and psychological deficits, has been accepted as a form of temporary insanity in a number of jurisdictions. This has been used as a defence in violent assaults, and in a few cases even murder, carried out by women. Clearly there is a gender asymmetry in the application of this defence, for although there is some evidence for monthly mood swings in males, this cannot be related so directly to major physiological changes. Therefore one of the basic tenets of the law that all are equal before it is not fully endorsed by the advocacy of this defence.

A rather more equitable syndrome, typically associated with women victims but potentially applicable to men, is rape trauma syndrome (RTS). This has parallels to PTSD, although it has a rather different emphasis and is not so clearly defined. The utility in court is to clarify why it may be that a rape victim would delay reporting the assault. The proposal from RTS is that the delay could initially indicate some doubt about the victim's own role in the rape, even possibly blaming herself. This has been claimed as part of the psychological effects of the trauma of the attack itself, which often include depression, suicidal thoughts, and general fear and anxiety.

An important point about these psychological consequences of various stressors and traumas is that they can result from events that do not involve obvious, extreme violence. Fear and profound psychological insult can be as traumatic, or even more so, than vicious physical aggression. Many studies show that stress relates to lack of control, and as a consequence situations that take feelings of personal control away from the individual can have significant impact on feelings of self-worth and ability to be in charge of one's life.

The psychology of the courtroom

The evidence given by forensic psychologists as expert witnesses in legal proceedings derives very largely from the assessment of individuals using clinical interviews and diagnostic instruments. This contrasts with a growing application of psychology to studying and influencing what happens in court, which tends

7. The more informal setting of a family tribunal

to draw more directly on social psychology than on clinical psychology or psychometric tests. As in so many other areas of the applications of psychology, the lead in this area has been taken in the USA. A major reason for this is that the American legal system is much more open to examination and allows much more intervention by attorneys than is the case in the UK. In particular, in some states it is possible to explore directly how juries actually make decisions. In most countries with juries, the workings of the jury are kept secret (although in France the judge often sits in on the jury's decision-making to ensure they are carrying out their task appropriately). This general secrecy does mean that very little is known about how the random sample of local people who make up a jury do deal with the evidence presented in a trial to reach a verdict.

The other major differences in the USA are the rules that allow attorneys to influence who may be a member of a jury. Although all adversarial legal systems permit some degree of selection of juries, this is usually constrained, but in the USA jurors can be questioned extensively and the courts tolerate many being excluded. This has given rise to 'scientific jury selection' in which psychologists guide attorneys to select juries that are most likely to find in support of their case. This may be followed up with advice on how to get the jury to accept the arguments put before them. Whether this distorts the legal process or is in fact any different from what attorneys do already is a matter of debate. The discussion is whether ethical boundaries may be crossed by what some consider to be interference with the normal jury process. It is therefore no surprise that many professionals have deep disquiet about this form of advice.

The guidance given to attorneys draws on attempts to understand how juries operate and the social and psychological processes that influence the decisions they make. Many general psychological questions arise in relation to jury decision-making. These include both issues of individual attitudes towards and understanding of what is presented to them in court, as well as social processes of influence. In the classic film *Twelve Angry Men*, the social psychology of the jury room is brilliantly illustrated when the character portrayed by Henry Fonda manages to sway the eleven other members of the jury.

These processes have particular poignancy when the jury makes a decision about the sentence that should be handed out. This can relate to compensation payments or in some murder cases in the USA whether the defendant should get the death penalty. Studies of jury decision-making show that attitudes towards the issues at hand, especially general attitudes towards the acceptability of the death penalty, can have much greater significance than any evidence presented in court.

One important point that does emerge from studies of juries is just how little they understand of the instructions given to them. This is due to a combination of the alienating aspects of the language of the law, the complexity of the issues being explored, and differences between jurors in their educational levels, prejudices, and pre-existing beliefs about the law. For example, in

Scotland jurors are given a document written in archaic legal jargon that describes the charge the defendant is facing. This tends to make the jurors more likely to believe the defendant is guilty than when the same information is given to them in a simple statement in everyday English.

The courts are of course aware of the challenges posed by these weaknesses, and psychologists are attempting to find more effective ways for attorneys and judges to interact with juries. This includes using analysis of instructions to take account of the educational level such instructions assume, providing special verdict forms for juries to complete, and even flow charts that can guide juries in how to explore the evidence and reach a decision. But the power of legal traditions slows down the speed with which such innovations can be implemented.

Jury selection, especially in the USA, attempts to deal directly with the crucial problem of bias in a juror. The idea that the jury will make an honest, objective judgement of the facts before them is undermined if a juror is so prejudiced to crucial issues in a case that he or she will ignore the facts and decide on the basis of pre-existing beliefs. It is around this argument that jury selection consultants are being drawn on by attorneys.

Trial tactics manuals have been drawn up to help attorneys identify biases in jurors that will prime them to be against their side of the argument. These give guidance on the questions that are legally acceptable to ask jurors before the trial starts and ways in which answers to those questions may indicate the biases a juror may have, such as the tendency for older people to be more likely to convict. However, this simple tactic may backfire when in some cases older people are more sympathetic to the defendant. Even the assumption that jurors will tend to be more lenient towards people who are the same ethnicity as themselves does not find general support in the research. There can be a tendency for people to feel the defendant is letting their ethnic group down, sometimes known as the 'black sheep effect'.

Slightly more effective in predicting the decision a juror will make are personality traits and attitudes. The possibility of giving jurors questionnaires to complete has led to attempts to develop standardized instruments that will, for instance, predict the likelihood that a juror will convict. The Juror Bias Scale is one such questionnaire. It asks whether or not the juror agrees with statements such as 'Generally, the police make an arrest only when they are sure about who committed the crime', or 'If a suspect runs from the police, then he probably committed the crime'. This does relate very loosely to the verdict that an individual may reach, but many factors in the case can mask this effect.

It may be reassuring to realize that, generally, attempts by psychologists to influence the outcome of cases through jury selection and guidance to attorneys have not been as powerful as those who wish to make a living from this consultancy sometimes claim. It is still the strength of the evidence that is by far the strongest predictor of the outcome of a case. However, when the evidence is very strong, the defendant is more likely to confess. So jury trials are more likely in cases where the evidence is more evenly balanced. In such situations, therefore, relatively small influences from the characteristics of the jurors or how the case is put before them may make the difference between a verdict of guilty or not guilty.

Conclusion

Legal procedures and principles pre-date scientific psychology by at least 2,000 years. It should therefore come as no surprise that, in general, lawyers are reluctant to embrace input from psychologists. As a consequence, the tendency has been for psychological evidence to be allowed initially for some very specific purpose, notably in pleas of insanity or competence to stand trial.

Over the last quarter of a century, these contributions have broadened so that, for instance, aspects of 'temporary insanity' may be adduced by drawing on psychological syndromes, notably PTSD.

This involvement with the courts broadened out to help explain what might otherwise seem as surprising behaviour, such as a woman staying with an abusive partner, or delaying in reporting a sexual assault. But once psychologists were allowed in as experts, their advice has continued to reach out to ever more aspects of the legal processes, now commenting on a variety of other aspects of court procedure. This has been as diverse as helping to select a jury that will be predisposed in a desired direction, or suggesting ways in which information should be presented in court.

All of these interactions between psychology and the courts are an interplay between two very different cultures. Forensic psychologists look to develop and use standardized tests and clinical interview procedures that place individuals within a generic framework. In contrast, the courts seek to get to grips with a given person and the particularities of a given case. Furthermore, the possibilities for psychological contributions are shaped by the details of the particular legal processes, which vary across jurisdictions. When the courts do not have juries, the scope for psychologists is much greater; however, their input is dealt with much more cautiously. The professionals involved in magisterial proceedings feel more able to take or leave any input from experts. Whilst many of those in the legal profession would regard it as arguable whether either set-up is greatly enhanced by drawing upon the current state of scientific psychology, there can be little doubt that the influence of psychology on court proceedings is growing rapidly around the world.

Chapter 5
Working with offenders

Forensic psychologists will most usually be found, not in court giving evidence, certainly not as part of a police investigation team, but working with convicted offenders. This may be in prisons, but there are also many other settings which incarcerate or control offenders and may attempt to change or rehabilitate them. People sentenced by the courts find their way into many places beyond jail, including probation services, therapeutic communities, and various forms of mental hospital or secure unit.

In all these settings, psychologists are involved in one of three broad tasks that can be thought of as focusing on different stages of the offender's life: past, present, or future.

- One set of roles for forensic psychology has the objective of helping the offender to deal with pre-existing problems that may have been a direct cause of their unacceptable actions, such as an inability to manage their own aggression, or contributory factors to their criminality such as drug or alcohol addiction, or even some longer-term problem like mental illness or personality disorder.
- Another set of roles is a form of counselling to assist the offender to cope with his current circumstances, for example reducing the risk of suicide in prison or helping people to cope who have recently been given a life sentence.

- The most common role, however, sits under the broad heading of 'risk assessment and management'. That is, trying to determine what risks the individual poses to himself and others, and what the most appropriate way of managing those risks are. These assessments may relate to managing these individuals within a specific institution or determining the risk if they are to be allowed out into the community at large.

Given the broad remit of present-day psychology, there are also an increasing number of psychologists who are providing guidance to the penal organizations in which they work at a more strategic level, often helping to select or train staff or to set in motion various programmes of work with offenders. In all of this work, as with all the other settings in which forensic psychologists operate, they contribute more than a knowledge-base about criminals. Many of the institutions in which they work may have an ingrained set of attitudes and a culture that is fundamentally punitive, not informed by any sort of university-level education or scientific approach to solving problems. Forensic psychologists may therefore often be the one professional group that gives most emphasis to an evidence-base for their work. The strength of that evidence, however, may often be open to considerable discussion.

Assessment

Any attempt to work with offenders will start with some form of assessment. This is really a classical medical framework in which a diagnosis of the patient's problems are recorded as a basis for determining what the most appropriate form of treatment is. However, in a psychological context it will be rare these days to look for any specific cause of the offender's actions, such as a particular mental abnormality, or a specific experience of sexual abuse as a child, but rather to try and gain some broader understanding of all aspects of that individual and his life that are relevant. After all, there are plenty of people who suffer

8. Working with an offender in prison

particular traumas who do not become offenders. It is therefore important to understand the full milieu out of which the offending has grown.

Extreme examples help to illustrate the complexity of the processes that need to be explored. Fred West was guilty of killing at least twenty young women over as many years before he was caught in 1994. He and his wife Rose sexually and physically abused these young women before killing them and burying them in the garden of their house and under their notorious patio. What would a forensic psychology assessment have revealed of Fred West if one had been carried out before he killed himself in prison?

The first and most obvious point was that he was virtually illiterate and probably learning disabled. Certainly the police assigned an 'appropriate adult' to be with him throughout their interviews because they feared he may not be able to fully understand the implications of what was happening to him within the legal process. Some indication of this may be found in his comments, when told that a body had been found under his patio, that the police should be careful how they put the paving back. His further request, once it was clear that he had committed murder, that he should now be allowed home may have been dark irony, but was perhaps more likely to be his lack of awareness of just how serious the situation was.

If the psychologist were able to get West to talk about his upbringing, she would probably become aware of how sexualized it was. West did write a sort of memoir before he killed himself and, although this seems to have been intended as a portrayal of the innocent, loving life he lived, he indicates, in passing, that his father had sex with West's daughter and that sexual activity generally was a prevalent part of family life. The crucial point is that West does not seem to recognize the destructive quality of all this, taking it much more for granted than most people would.

In addition to his acceptance of untrammelled sexual gratification quite early on, in his teens he raped a young woman but managed to avoid being convicted of this crime. The stage was thus set for a continuation of this predatory activity. His patterns of behaviour and attitudes were ingrained within a view of himself that was shaped in part by the way his parents and others in his family treated him. It is even possible that his only feeling of being at all significant came when he was sexually violent.

Even these precursors in parental role models, deep-seated attitudes, and a limited understanding of the consequences of his actions may not have turned him into a serial killer. It was when he got together with Rose, who had a background in crime and prostitution, that he was encouraged to take his depredations further. Together they created an environment that made sexual violence and murder a way of life.

9. An offender being assessed

Working with violent sex offenders

Clearly, Fred West would have been a challenge to any attempt to 'treat' his condition. But for a person who was less vulnerable and whose destructive life experiences had been less long-lasting and less intense, many prison psychologists would hope some programmes could be put in place that would at the very least reduce the risk of future offending. These programmes have in common the recognition that the causes of offending will vary from one person to another and will be multifaceted. The offender will therefore be helped to deal with a number of aspects of himself, his actions, and his lifestyle.

Typically, the programmes that help offenders develop a lifestyle that is more socially acceptable are built around group sessions in which various aspects of the conditions that give rise to the violence are explored. These will include role-playing as well as intense discussions. The purpose is to help the participants develop more empathy for their victims and more insight into their own attitudes. In addition, they are alerted to the conditions that give rise to their offending so that they can examine them and avoid them.

These interactions can last over many months and be very intensive, but there are many difficulties in delivering such programmes in prison. Not least of these difficulties is that prisons are strange institutions. It is rare for there to be any mixture of the sexes, and alcohol is banned. There is not the normal mix of general activities, with prisoners being locked in their cells from early evening until the following morning. How can you train, treat, or rehabilitate people to live normal existences in such an abnormal environment? Indeed, there may be aspects of prison life that are more likely to drag offenders into an increasing spiral of crime. It is often claimed, for instance, that illegal narcotics are more readily available in prison than outside. But there is also the simple fact that prisoners are mixing with convicted criminals all day. The social influence of these other offenders cannot be overestimated.

In addition, offenders are incarcerated because of profoundly entrenched ways of dealing with the world. They will usually have some strong self-justification for what they did, and a proportion will deny the crime ever happened, or that it happened the way it was presented to obtain a conviction. These denials and justifications can be tackled directly by psychologists in meetings with the offender, but if the offender refuses to accept the alternative interpretation of his actions then a quite different approach to treatment is needed. This may centre on helping the offender develop positive skills and become less vulnerable to being caught up in illegal situations.

One of the big risks is that offenders will feel coerced into participating without ever being openly antagonistic. There are plenty of accounts of this producing situations in which the psychologist has assumed that progress is being made, only to discover later that the offender has merely learned what it was necessary to say to complete the programme, without ever changing their attitudes or subsequent behaviour. Some studies show this clearly, with those psychopaths who were rated as having done very well in therapy being the ones most likely to offend in the future.

One attempt to get around some of these problems is to create what are known as 'therapeutic communities'. Convicted men have to apply to join these communities and demonstrate to the community their desire to really change. The whole institution runs on an intensive soul-searching basis so that there is no room for play-acting or hiding. Such communities are extremely expensive to run and also have to be highly selective in who they can work with, even though some studies suggest they may be more effective than any other form of intervention with serious offenders.

Such intensive interventions are typically kept alive and effective by a charismatic manager, being almost a form of focused cult. This can give rise to some bizarre establishments. One often-quoted example is of a community in the late 1980s that had eighty hours of therapy each week. This gave hardly any time for leisure or more directly beneficial training in skills. Apparently, it also included a fortnight in a self-contained chamber where food and drink was provided from pipes in the walls. Along the way, the inmates were made to use a variety of psychotropic drugs, such as LSD. People were expected to participate for two whole years and were not allowed out until they could show they had complied with what the 'treatment' was expected to achieve. Perhaps not surprisingly, people identified as psychopaths before they joined this community were actually more dangerous and disturbed after the therapy than before.

Alcoholics and other substance dependants

Perhaps more success has been achieved with treatment interventions for reducing dependency on alcohol and other drugs. This has the knock-on effect of reducing addicts' offending as well. The effectiveness of these interventions may be partially due to the focused nature of the behaviours that are to be changed. This allows a clear identification of the stages the participants need to go through if they are to reduce their drug dependence. Such programmes probably owe a lot to the initiative of Alcoholics Anonymous, which relies on a mixture of group support and acceptance of the challenges that are faced by addicts. The emphasis on the consequences for others of the addict's actions also helps to develop attitudes, beliefs, and understanding that can sustain the offender once outside prison.

Enhanced thinking skills

In contrast to the Alcoholics Anonymous view that the alcoholic cannot really get rid of his addiction but has to learn to manage it 'one day at a time', it is widely accepted in psychology that the way to change behaviour is first to change the way a person thinks about events, and then to set in motion actions that are derived from those changed thought patterns. This can only be done in gentle stages that have to be carefully worked out and wherever possible tuned to the particular individual. In a nutshell, this is what is called cognitive behavioural therapy (CBT). This underlies many of the intervention programmes for working with sex offenders and addicts, but also is relevant to broader problems that offenders have to deal with, such as the management of their anger.

A typical example of how this may be explored with an offender would be to take a possible, or actual, incident in their current prison experience that is potentially strongly emotional. In a group session or a one-to-one therapy session, the offender may be asked to consider a situation in which they go to the visitors' room at 3.00pm, expecting a visit from their partner, but after waiting 15 minutes she has still not arrived. The prisoner may report that his immediate thought is that she has dropped him for someone else, become angry about that, with associated feelings of nausea, and go back to the wing determined to give her a piece of his mind over the phone that evening.

It would be pointed out to him how unhelpful that is and that he has drifted into 'automatic thoughts' that generate feelings and actions that are very unproductive and potentially destructive. Alternatives would then be elicited, such as thinking that perhaps his partner had got stuck in traffic, which would have kept him in an optimistic mood, feeling more comfortable. In such a state, he could wait quietly, perhaps having a chat with prison staff about a recent football game. Then if she did turn up, he would be in a good state to be with her. If she did not, he would not have suffered and could still talk to her later about why, without that conversation being too harsh.

This approach to helping prisoners develop the ability to have more positive thoughts, and consequently more positive feelings and actions, has been developed into specific, organized programmes. There are a number of these which are evaluated and accredited in the UK so that they can be delivered in a standard, reliable format across the prison system. The most frequently run course deals with enhanced thinking skills (ETS). It runs over 22 hour-long sessions with associated 'out of session assignments' that are rather like homework. The course runs on a group basis and consists of a mixture of explanations of the basic psychological ideas behind CBT, explorations of the particular experiences of group members, development of social skills such as listening and asking for help, and a number of exercises that help participants to experience and act on what is discussed in the group.

Evaluating interventions

For such interventions to be regarded as scientific and supported by evidence, it is necessary to evaluate them. This is not as straightforward as it may seem. For a start, how do you measure the consequence of the interventions? If the programme deals with anger management or drug misuse, this needs to be assessed before and after. This is not easy when the activity can occur in many different settings or is illegal, but if the intention is to reduce consequent crime, that also needs to be monitored. The challenge to all programmes is that they may just make the offenders more able to avoid detection rather than to offend less. In some cases, an attempt is made to equate the cost to the community of actions before 'treatment' with the costs after. This looks neat when bureaucrats present the results to politicians in a bid to keep the funding for any project, but a moment's thought will reveal how difficult it is to put a cost on all the implications of criminal activity.

Nonetheless, despite these challenges, a number of studies report that for the drug-dependency programmes there is some evidence that they eventually help to reduce acquisitive crime to one-third or more of what it was before people participated. The more general enhanced thinking skills courses also produce statistically significant improvements in behaviour, typically reducing recidivism by about 20%.

The question, however, arises as to whether this change was some form of maturation that would have happened anyway. There are real practical and ethical problems in randomly assigning participants to 'treatment' and 'non-treatment' as would be done in a double-blind experimental, pharmaceutical trial, so comparisons have to be made with other groups that do not experience the interventions. In general, it is found that those who go through these carefully organized programmes do better when compared with those who do not, as well as the before/after differences, but this is all relative. Many offenders do not give up their drug habits and criminal lifestyles, but overall, fewer are involved in crime after these programmes and their drug habits tend to be milder.

Personality disorder

There is one set of behavioural problems on which such 'treatment' programmes may have little impact. This received international significance when in 1998, Michael Stone was convicted of brutally killing Dr Lin Russell and her six-year-old daughter, and of attempting to murder her other daughter, nine-year-old Josie, in broad daylight, for no apparent reason. It emerged that he had a history of violence, growing up in a dysfunctional family, being moved from one residential institution to another. He had spent time in prison and been assessed for mental illness because of his violence. His sister reported that prior to the murders, Stone had sought help for his fantasies of killing someone. But although he was receiving some treatment for his anxieties, it had not been possible for anyone to assign a medical diagnosis of any form of mental illness that would allow him to be hospitalized. Subsequent consideration of the circumstances surrounding the murders and Stone's own background pointed to his being a bomb about to explode, yet no one seemed able to do anything about it.

The problem of preventing Stone from doing further harm had two components. One is that he had not carried out any crime at that time for which he could be arrested. The second was that he could not be given a medical diagnosis that would allow him to be committed to a mental hospital or other secure setting. There are a number of people who fall into this no-man's-land between the law and psychiatry, who present very real potential for violence but for whom until recently there was no formal management procedure. This can include people due out of prison at the end of their sentence who are talking of harming themselves and/or others. Or men who have a long history abusing children and who are now applying to be moved to a more open hospital setting than the very secure units in which they are currently housed. Slightly different are men who are on remand, waiting for their court case to be heard, who admit to sexual excitement from violence and, say, high-speed dangerous driving.

All of these people are in contact with reality. They do not hallucinate, hearing voices or having visions, nor do they have delusions, believing they are God or the prime minister. They may not have extreme swings of mood from elation to depression. There may be little or no substance abuse in their background, but it is clear that, at the very least, they are strange people. They will typically find it very difficult to form deep, lasting relationships, lacking empathy for others, they will react emotionally in quite inappropriate ways and may be very impulsive. In their milder forms, any of these characteristics may be found in the 'average' person. They are thus regarded as reflecting a disorder of the personality rather than of the mind.

In the way of clinical diagnosis, ten different forms of personality disorder have been identified, running from the paranoid to the obsessive-compulsive. They cluster around eccentricity, emotionality, and anxiety. But the individuals who are of concern because of their potential for violence are those in the 'emotional' cluster, typically classified as having 'antisocial personality disorder', or the oddly labelled 'borderline personality disorder'.

This is an intriguing area of the diagnosis of mental disorder and one rife with controversy. Consider the official list of criteria for the diagnosis of antisocial personality disorder, derived from the Diagnostic and Statistical Manual of Mental Disorders (DSM-IV):

Shows a pervasive disregard for the rights of others, as indicated by at least three of:

Repeated illegal behaviour
Evidence of conduct disorder before the age of fifteen
Repeated lying or cheating for profit or pleasure
Impulsivity

Aggressiveness
Disregard for safety
Irresponsibility
Lack of remorse.

Surely this describes a typical, chronic criminal? What does it add
to give the pattern of characteristics a label that sits within a
Diagnostic and Statistical Manual of Mental Disorders, which also
contains such diagnoses as schizophrenia and depression?

Many authorities would claim that all the label of personality
disorder adds is a patina which implies some coherent set of
characteristics that indicates the person is unusual and not
mentally ill, but little else. For those trying to manage such
potentially dangerous individuals, it offers the safety net of a
'diagnosis' to defend how these people are dealt with. Indeed, for
some of the people so diagnosed it is a relief to be told they have
a 'disorder' rather than just being nasty people. But the main
pressure to use the personality disorder diagnosis comes from
outside the medical profession. It is politicians who want to avoid
the embarrassment of cases like the murder of Lin Russell and
her daughter who warm to the idea that potential offenders
could obtain a diagnosis that would allow them to be put in an
institution. In the UK, a label of 'dangerous and severe personality
disorder' has been created and special units set up that aim to work
with people so diagnosed. The objective is to help them eventually
move into more conventional, secure units and possibly even on
from there back into the community.

The assumption that is the foundation of this approach is that it
is possible to change the consequences of a disorder of
a personality. The favoured method is to create intensive
therapeutic communities. But letting people move on from such
communities is a high-risk strategy. It only needs one 'graduate' to
kill once he has been let out for the whole process to be brought
into disrepute by public outrage. These communities are therefore

more likely to operate as relatively benign prisons in which the inmates have indeterminate sentences. This is an extremely controversial approach because, sadly, there is a long history in many countries of people being institutionalized for what they *might* do rather than for what they have done.

Coping with prison

The objectives of imprisonment vary from country to country and from one time to another. Sometimes the view is that prisons are there to improve the behaviour of inmates. This aim is captured in the euphemistic US label for prisons as 'correctional facilities'. Sometimes they are seen as purely for punishment and as a way to deter offending. But what most people accept is that prisons should at least not make people any worse or any more of a risk to society. This latter aim is not so easy to achieve. Psychologists who work in prisons are therefore often concerned with what the debilitating effects might be on the inmates and how they may be mitigated. The attention is usually on the prisoners, but some would also suggest that the staff, who spend their working lives in these institutions, should also be considered.

Studies have demonstrated that there are a number of psychological changes in prisoners as a result of coping with prison life. These include:

- becoming reliant on the staff and others to make decisions for them;
- suspicion and distrust of others, with possibly neurotic alertness;
- developing a mask to hide their feelings which makes relating to others difficult;
- reduced belief in having any personal significance;
- re-activating childhood traumas that had similar consequences.

For people who have mental illness, or who are intellectually very limited and do not have external support from family or friends, these debilitating effects can be extreme. In some cases, especially when external factors, such as the breakdown of a relationship, intrude into the experience in prison, then the psychological challenges can be so great that prisoners commit suicide or self-harm.

As is their wont, forensic psychologists have developed scales that assess the risk of suicide or self-harm, drawing on what is known about the prisoner, his background, and current experiences. These assessments are used to guide management of the offenders and in some cases to provide support and counselling. But it is still the case that men in prison are about five times more likely to kill themselves than those outside, with about one a week killing themselves in UK prisons and a similar number in Californian and Texan prisons.

Assessing and managing risk

The prediction of various forms of risk, of harming oneself or of harming others, of future sexual offending or other forms of criminal activity, has become a major, and extremely challenging, task for forensic psychologists in many different settings. A number of risk-assessment tools have therefore been developed over the last quarter of a century. One of the most useful is a structured checklist used by a trained professional, such as the twenty-item Historical/Clinical/Risk management scale (HCR-20).

The HCR-20 combines what may be regarded as 'static', relatively unchanging, factors and more 'dynamic' factors that are potentially open to change. The static factors will tend to be historical, such as the offender's previous violence, employment problems, clear evidence of psychopathy, and substance abuse. The dynamic factors will be more directly psychological issues such as lack of insight, impulsivity, and unfeasible plans for the future. In addition, matters of social support and the way the individual has dealt with any forms of remedial intervention, as well as potential stressors, can all be taken into account.

The consequence of such assessments is interestingly revealed if we compare two different offenders. One is a married man in his mid-30s who has pleaded guilty to sexually abusing his teenage daughter since she was 4 years old. The other is a young man in his early 20s who was convicted of having sex with an underage boy whom he had just met in a local park.

According to some standard risk-assessment procedures, particularly the Static-99, the young man has a much higher risk of future offending than the married man. The reason is that being married, over 25, and offending within the family on a female are less predictive of future offences than are having had no cohabiting relationship, offending against a stranger and a male. This difference may come as some surprise, but it is based on studies using these assessment procedures and following up their predictive validity.

However, although such assessments have a strong logic to them, and studies show that they are broadly prognostic, they are far from being foolproof. One simple reason for this is that, although it may be possible to characterize an individual, it is much more difficult to characterize and predict the situations in which he will find himself. Also, for many people who must be assessed there may be little reliable background information. One general principle, though, is a simple one. The more recently a person has been violent in the past, the more likely he is to be violent in the near future. For these reasons, it does appear that, like weather forecasts, it is possible to predict what is likely to happen in the next 48 hours, or even 14 days, but much less feasible for longer timescales such as 48 months or 14 years.

Victimology

One point it is easy to miss in discussions of working with offenders is that many of them are also victims. Therefore the development of studies of victims has relevance both to offenders and those they offend against. Such studies are fraught with demands for careful presentation. They show that not all people are equally likely to become victims, but it is all too easy for this to appear to imply that victims carry some responsibility for the crimes they suffer. This is certainly not the intention of such studies.

What these studies explore is what makes people particularly vulnerable to becoming victims. This covers such matters as whether in acquisitive crime the property is in particularly high demand, or whether the person themselves can be seen as especially 'attractive' to a potential offender in a number of different ways. In addition, the proximity of possible criminals increases the risk of becoming a target. The person's actual physical or psychological vulnerability is a further issue. If they are very young, old, weak, or have learning disabilities, then under exposed conditions they may be more likely to suffer an offence. All of these issues have implications for how vulnerable people can be protected, whether they are offenders within prison or law-abiding citizens outside.

Conclusions: the problem of prison

The range of possible locations where offenders may be sent throws into high relief serious and challenging questions as to what are the purposes of prison and other ways of managing convicted men and women, and how successful the various strategies are in achieving their objectives. Different countries have different conceptualizations of what the purpose of prison is and the conditions under which it should be used as a way of dealing with offenders. Psychologists have been at the forefront of this debate in exploring the impact of prison and setting in motion an increasing range of interventions with offenders in and out of prison as attempts to change them.

Psychological and physical maturation with related adjustments, such as settling with a partner and having children and opportunities for acceptable legitimate careers, are the most likely lifestyle changes that lead to offenders stepping out of criminality. Some are taken off the list of offenders because they become so entrenched in criminality that their life is spent in prison. The cynical view may thus be that any attempt at rehabilitation is little more than a holding process whilst individuals grow old enough to accept the error of their ways or to lack the physical prowess or related psychological skills to carry out crimes, or avoid detection.

Although there are without doubt people who have benefited from being in prison, especially when that is associated with treatment programmes and other forms of education and training, there is a fundamental problem in using prison as a place for rehabilitation. It is so unlike any other setting in which a person may have to cope, with the possible exception of certain military or religious environments. Therefore the application of psychology has to cover both the support for staff as well as monitoring the environment, in order to ensure the prison runs smoothly ('keeping the wheels on' as a police officer friend of mine graphically described it). There will also be work in helping prisoners to deal with the demanding and strange environment in which they find themselves. No civilized society should allow prisoners to get so depressed that they kill themselves.

Various programmes and courses are finding currency in prisons as ways of helping prisoners to become worthy citizens. Most of the successful ones are based on some aspect of cognitive behavioural therapy. This requires the offender to change how he thinks about crucial matters, such as women or potential victims, as well as changing how he acts. The difficulty of such programmes is that they have to be assessed to some degree on the basis of what the offender says and of what he is subsequently arrested for. It is always possible that he will just learn the right things to say and how to avoid being caught.

When an offender has some distinct mental illness, the challenge of helping him may be regarded more as a form of treatment. In many countries, such people are incarcerated in institutions that are established as secure hospitals, even though their staff are likely to be members of a prison officers' union. Such institutions pose very particular challenges at both the organizational and personal levels.

A powerful aspect of such attempts at rehabilitation is the recognition that the offender is probably a victim too and may need help to deal with his own traumatic experiences. However, the processes for helping victims are most active with people who are not offenders and relate to a growing area that has been labelled 'victimology'. This examines whether there are aspects of people that make them more likely to become victims, as well as developing ways of helping victims handle their experiences.

In order to let people out of prison on parole, or more particularly from secure hospitals where their sentence may be indefinite until they are deemed safe to allow back into the community, a careful assessment has to be made of how dangerous the person is. Psychologists have attempted to develop systematic procedures to make such assessments, but they are fraught with difficulties.

Chapter 6
Working with law enforcement

It is often assumed that forensic psychology is an integrated part of police work, but in fact law enforcement is probably the most recent domain into which psychologists have ventured. You might expect that a study of the causes of criminality would play a significant part in preparation for being a police officer, and that understanding criminals more generally would be integrated into their training. The fact is that around the world police training has usually focused on the study of the law and police procedures. It is really only since the 1990s that psychology has begun to find its way into the work of law-enforcement agencies. This has probably been stimulated by the great interest in 'offender profiling' – the idea that the psychologist acts like a latter-day Sherlock Holmes, solving criminal mysteries with his profound insights into human nature. While such fiction is exciting, it exaggerates and distorts reality. It also draws on only a very limited aspect of what the police do and of the way in which psychologists contribute to their work, as we shall see in this chapter.

Investigative procedure

In a typical detective story, there is a small handful of possible suspects from amongst whom the investigators must chose.

Often, the possible villains are limited by the device of them all being in an isolated house, on a boat, a train, or in a small secluded community. Even when there is a much larger pool from which suspects can be drawn, the demands of a manageable storyline require that the police will find their way to the villain by a relatively direct set of stages. There may be leaps along the way, often produced by an interesting character within or outside the police. Today, this person is likely to be some sort of scientist or 'profiler'. Crime fiction rarely reveals the steady, painstaking, labour-intensive search through records and other sources of information that is typical of most major enquiries. Neither does crime fiction illustrate, as one detective mentioned to me with some feeling, the great amount of paperwork and form-filling that police officers have to do.

In real cases, when there is no obvious suspect, detectives have to go through a number of stages before they can bring the most likely person to court. They have to decide where to look for possible culprits and generate lists of possible offenders. For example, they may search police records for people who have committed similar crimes in the past, or they may review all known associates of any victim, or people who may have a reason for committing the crime. Then, they must winnow this list down to a manageable number for careful scrutiny. This might include checking whether any of the suspects were in prison at the time of the offence, known to be out of the country, or had died without this being in their records. The names on this distilled list then have to be put into some sort of order of priority so that very intensive examinations can be carried out on each possible suspect, determining if they had valid alibis or other evidence that they did not commit the crime.

All of these stages involve collecting information, making some sense of it, and acting on its implications. In other words, a cycle of stages that is repeated until the case is solved. The first stage is one in which information becomes available that a crime has, or

10. Photograph of a murder crime scene

may have been, committed. This information is often ambiguous. Even if a man is discovered standing over a dead body holding a gun, investigators still need to prove to the satisfaction of the courts that the man intentionally fired the gun to kill the victim. In other cases, there may be more complex and challenging interpretation of the facts.

These many aspects of an investigation – collecting the facts, making sense of them, and managing the actions that are needed to follow their implications – are open to assistance from psychologists. As they have moved into this broad array of activities, a new area of applied psychology has emerged which I called 'investigative psychology'. The label seems to have stuck, and an increasing number of police forces around the world have set up investigative psychology units, and it has become part of the syllabus of many university courses.

Improving the organization of information

Police investigations are built around information. This information may involve records of previous crimes or criminals, observations from surveillance, photographs of crime scenes, or interviews with victims, witnesses, or suspects. As scientists, psychologists are used to collecting information and sorting it out. There are therefore many ways in which they are helping investigators to be more effective in their data-collection procedures.

A simple example is that instead of a police officer going to a house following a burglary and making a note of anything he thinks important, he will be provided with a carefully developed checklist. Preparing such a checklist can benefit enormously from the century or so of expertise that psychologists have in questionnaire design. Only a few police forces have taken advantage of this, and there are as a consequence many such checklists in place that are cumbersome, ambiguous, and that do not have the reliability properties that would be expected of a recording instrument developed by psychologists. But the police are becoming aware of such challenges. One senior officer calculated that for his force, they had to employ one more person for every extra piece of information they collected. Therefore an efficient data-collection protocol is of direct financial benefit.

Improving interviewing

Central to police work are interviews with witnesses, victims, and suspects. Even the 'stop and search' procedure, or finding out what has happened in a traffic accident, requires the police officer to ask questions and record the answers. The interview is a fundamentally psychological process based on personal interactions, so there has been a great deal of research exploring how interviews can be improved in many different situations. This has given rise in England and Wales to standard police interview procedures which are rooted in a psychological analysis of what happens in an interview.

Two related processes are considered as at the heart of interviewing. One draws on the fact that, typically, what is happening in an investigative interview is that the interviewee is trying to remember what has happened. The other is the relationship between the interviewer and interviewee that allows an open and honest account to be given.

Remembering was one of the first psychological processes to be explored as psychology emerged from medicine and philosophy. These studies showed, as we noted earlier, that memory is not a passive fading of a trace, like a watercolour painting that has been kept in the sun, in which memories become ever vaguer over time. Rather, it is a reconstructive process that utilizes a mixture of experiences. It is essentially an active cognitive process. Therefore a procedure known as the 'cognitive interview' has gained currency to help improve witnesses' memory for events. It consists of a number of suggestions:

- create a feeling of mutual understanding;
- listen to what is being said in an active, attentive manner;
- allow the respondent to recall as freely as possible;
- make sure questions are open-ended, not allowing a simple yes/no answer;
- take time to make sense of responses, pausing if necessary;
- do not interrupt the flow of response;
- check the details of the account that is given;
- try to recreate the original context of the events being described.

Laboratory studies have shown that these procedures do give rise to a lot more information, but the extent to which that information is of real value to an investigation is more difficult to determine. These studies also tend to undervalue that second crucial aspect of an interview: the relationship between the interviewer and interviewee. In the clinical surroundings of a university experiment, there are not the same tensions and preconceptions that are present when a witness is seated in a police interview room. Establishing a supportive working relationship with the respondent and being able to nurse her along to reveal what she remembers is a social skill that police officers may be hard-pressed to develop.

When the interviewee is the suspect, matters become even more challenging. The cognitive interview assumes a willing respondent keen to remember as much as possible. This cannot be assumed for a suspect, although there will be occasions when he may genuinely need help remembering. Here the rapport with the interviewer may be crucial, but if the suspect is unwilling to cooperate the interview has to take a very different form.

Studies have explored which processes are most likely to encourage offenders to cooperate and, perhaps not unsurprisingly, indications are that it is how good the evidence is against them.

It is actually very rare for offenders to modify the account they give of events during the course of an interview. The frustration this causes the police is reflected in their desire to find ways of making offenders confess. In the USA, where the laws on what is allowable when interviewing a suspect are more relaxed than in the UK, strategies of cheating and coercing suspects are proposed. However, the risks of them producing false confessions so outweigh any possible probative value that their use has to be very carefully evaluated.

Eyewitness testimony

This challenge to the utility of what is reported by witnesses becomes especially important when an eyewitness is identifying a perpetrator. Such evidence can be very influential, especially in front of a jury. Yet, a number of studies over the last two decades has shown that eyewitness testimony can be flawed, even when eyewitnesses are very confident in their identification. It has been shown that beyond the more obvious limitations on the trustworthiness of eyewitness testimony, relating for example to how good the lighting was and how long they spent in the presence of the culprit, there are also aspects of the event itself that can distort the memory.

The most widely reported distortions come from what is called 'weapon focus'. This is the idea that if a weapon, such as a gun or knife, is involved, then a victim or witness will be almost mesmerized by having their attention drawn to the weapon and thus will not have noticed the features of the offender so readily. The trauma of the event can also have more general effects which may heighten a person's awareness of what was going on, and thus improve their memory, or focus their attention in ways that make identification difficult.

The details of the way in which identifications take place lend themselves to neat, laboratory-based studies. These do show

11. A police line-up

that witnesses can be unconsciously nudged into selecting the person whom those overseeing the procedure, such as in an identity parade, believe is the offender. Witnesses can also feel the pressure to make some sort of choice even if they are unsure, which can also lead to miscarriages of justice. These effects can be quite subtle, as in recent research showing that children were more likely to select someone in an identity parade if the person running the process was wearing a uniform than if he was not. Suggestions have therefore emerged about how eyewitness identifications should be conducted, for example that the person running the identification process should not know who the suspect actually is.

The fact that most of the research on interviewing and eyewitness testimony has used laboratory-based studies has over recent years led to debates about how much of what the studies reveal really can be applied to actual police investigations. The artificiality of the experiments has raised questions about their value in assisting enquiries. The problem is that, with the pressures of day-to-day policing, it is extremely difficult to set up many of the recommended procedures, whether it be cognitive interviews or special ways of running identity parades. Also, whilst it may be possible to control what happens with suspects and witnesses when they are in a police station, it is much more difficult to manage how they are dealt with outside of those confines, such as in the police car on the way to the police station.

Vulnerable witnesses

Some witnesses, or victims, may be regarded as particularly vulnerable to the pressures of the interview process. These can include children, people with learning disabilities, and the frail or elderly. Their understanding of the legal process they are part of, of the questions they are being asked, or of the events they are reporting may not be as great as would be expected of most adults. Vulnerable witnesses may also be more susceptible to influence from authority figures. There is also evidence that their memory for events is not likely to be as good as for the population in general.

A number of procedures have therefore been proposed for ensuring that these witnesses are not unduly influenced by the investigative or legal context. These include enhanced versions of the cognitive interview, and other specific guidelines on how the interview should be conducted. In court, the use of closed-circuit television is sometimes used with children so that they are not too overawed by the judicial process.

Detecting deception

Where the interviewee has reasons for not telling the truth or cooperating with the investigation, especially if he is the culprit, there is a need to detect deceit. This turns out to be much more difficult than is often appreciated, although techniques that rely on measuring the person's physiological response (lie detectors) have limited success in some circumstances. The challenge resides

12. A polygraph (lie detector) in use

in the need we all have from time to time not to tell the truth and therefore our general ability to be reasonably convincing liars. To take this a stage further, if a person believes what he is saying is the truth, then how he says it may not differ at all from when he gives a genuine account. In other words, lying is not some rare and strange behaviour that will inevitably have tell-tale signs associated with it.

There are nonetheless certain demands made on a person if he is to perpetuate a lie, and an understanding of these can be of value in detecting deception. The most obvious pressure on not telling the truth is that a lie has to be some form of invention. It requires an act of imagination. This is why experienced liars will build their fabrication on something that has actually happened, or they will avoid giving much information at all. The avoidance of telling the truth may therefore be one of the main indicators of deception; in other words, an unwillingness to answer or elaborate on the facts.

109

Once a person is prepared to give some account, then the most obvious way of determining its veracity is whether it is plausible and fits in with other known facts. Inconsistencies are a useful indicator, together with a lack of appropriate detail. Checklists have been prepared that are particularly valuable for examining written statements, helping to draw attention to the sorts of valid details that might be expected. These are used in some countries, notably Germany, especially for examining children's accounts of sexual abuse. The most frequently cited is statement validity analysis (SVA), which draws on criteria-based content analysis (CBCA). This makes use of 13 main criteria:

- logical consistency
- unstructured production
- quantity of detail
- contextual embedding
- description of interactions
- reproduction of conversation
- unexpected complications
- unusual details
- superfluous details
- attribution of respondent's mental state
- spontaneous corrections
- admitting lack of memory
- raising doubts

Emotional pressure when lying

The invention involved in lying, its 'cognitive load', as well as the implications of being caught out, can cause an emotional reaction in liars. It is this emotional response that more objective procedures for lie detection attempt to pick up. Some of the procedures claim to be able to use non-verbal cues such as fidgeting and speaking more slowly, but the problem here is that you have to know what is normal for that person. If he is normally fidgety and speaks slowly, then he may actually speak more rapidly when he is focusing on getting away with a lie.

Rather more success has been found with direct measures of emotional activation (known technically as 'arousal'). The best known of these, referred to as a 'lie detector', or 'polygraph', measures the respondent's arousal level on a number of indices at the same time, such as heart rate, breathing rate, and amount of sweating indicated in a galvanic skin response. These were originally a set of pens drawing the levels on a sheet of paper, which is why it was called a 'poly-graph'.

The process consists of asking a set of questions and then determining whether there is any obvious emotional response to some and not others. The most useful set of questions, known as the 'guilty knowledge test', consists of neutral questions, such as what the day of the week is, combined with questions that relate to things that only the person who was guilty would know, such as features of the crime scene. Studies show that such procedures can certainly help to support the case that the respondent is innocent, but are far less useful when indicating he may be guilty. In other words, not many innocent people appear guilty, but plenty of people who appear guilty are actually innocent. Intriguingly, one of the reported powers of the technique is that suspects who believe in its utility may often admit to their crimes as part of the polygraph process.

Other forms of questioning and techniques that claim to assess stress in acoustics of the voice (voice stress analysis) are also widely used, but with far less scientific evidence for their validity. Recently claims have also been made for procedures that make direct measures of brain activity, sometimes rather inaccurately called 'brain fingerprinting'. As with all the other procedures, their weaknesses founder on two issues. One is whether an effective and convincing rapport can be established between the interviewer and the respondent. The other is the way in which general levels of arousal caused by the interview process can mask genuine innocence. A further difficulty is that the focus on the response from the equipment may distract the interviewer from listening carefully to the account and so identifying confusions and inconsistencies in it.

Experiments may be set up in which the tester can use some physiological measure to reliably determine if subjects are telling the truth about which of a set of playing cards they are holding. This may be trumpeted by commercial companies selling the equipment to indicate its foolproof nature. But such 'lying' is far removed from a suspect indicating exactly what he was doing on the night of a murder.

Interviewing or interrogation?

Many police officers, and the public at large, sometimes think that the purpose for interviewing a suspect is to obtain a confession, or some crucial information, such as the names of associates. The term 'interrogation' is used with the implication of this objective. As a result, a mythology has grown up around the idea that psychologists can help interrogators, in popular parlance, 'to get a cough'. However, the great majority of psychologists consider this inappropriate, unethical, and probably foolhardy. One extreme indication of this has been an attempt within the American Psychological Association to have those psychologists who may have overseen the torture of detainees in Guantanamo Bay disqualified from practising.

So, although there have been proposals from ex-FBI agents and others on how to carry out an interview to obtain a confession, in general psychologists believe these are counter-productive. They can give rise to misleading information and generally sail too close to legal unacceptability to be worth the risk. Furthermore, as has been noted, the best way to obtain truthful information is to build up an appropriate relationship with the suspect and make it clear to him what the evidence is against him. If the evidence is not available, it may be better to put extra effort into obtaining it rather than relying on a coercive interview.

It is also the case that various attempts at using 'truth drugs', such as sodium amytal or sodium pentothal, suffer from the same problems as other coercive techniques. The interviewee may talk more, but can unknowingly mix fact and fantasy. Most jurisdictions regard their use as unacceptable and a form of torture.

The use of hypnosis as part of an enhanced interview technique does not suffer from the same problems as coercive forms of interrogation, and has been used successfully with witnesses. However, there is certainly no guarantee that what the subject reveals in an hypnotic state is the truth, or that it will be uninfluenced by the hypnotist. For this reason, there are strict guidelines in many countries on how forensic hypnosis should be carried out, and an appropriate reluctance to use it except in very special circumstances.

False allegations

False confessions are mentioned in Chapter 4, on courtroom psychology, but the converse of this, false allegations, are also a real challenge to police investigations. This may involve, for example, children alleging they were sexually abused, or older victims who falsely claim they were assaulted. With children, the issue can be explored using statement validity analysis, but this procedure may be less valid than many would wish.

Particularly contentious are allegations that emerge during the course of therapy and which are presented as memories that are recovered, as explained earlier. But there are many other cases, especially with allegations of rape and sexual harassment, in which it is extremely difficult to determine whether the claim is false. The difficulties come from social attitudes that have been buffeted by the appalling way in which victims of sexual assault were often dealt with in the past. This has led to a pendulum-swing in which it may be regarded as politically incorrect even to suggest that an allegation of rape could be false. However, there is some evidence that as many as one in three allegations of rape may not be valid, but without a great deal of sensitive scientific research, this is difficult to determine with any confidence. It relates, though, to the very small proportion of initial reports of rape that end in convictions.

Effective inferences and offender profiling

A second stage in the investigation process is making inferences on the basis of the information collected. These are suggestions as to where it would be fruitful to look for further information and what sorts of people or data may be most productive in solving the case. When the crime has been carried out in a manner that does not leave many direct clues, that is, when there is little forensic evidence that can be used like a twine that can be tugged to haul in the culprit, then detectives have to make some imaginative leaps to identify the offender. It is in these situations that the much-vaunted 'offender profile' often appears in fictional accounts of crimes.

In the 1980s, the label 'offender profiling' was given to the process of deriving hypotheses, from how a crime was carried out, about the sort of person who committed the crime. The most direct way of thinking about this process is that it is an attempt to take some of the explanations for why people commit crimes and in a sense run them backwards. So at its most elementary, if we think that brain damage leads someone to be violent and we are looking at a violent crime, then we might assume that the offender is someone who is brain-damaged. This example, though, reveals immediately difficulties in using many explanations for crime as a basis for making inferences about the offenders, as discussed in Chapter 2. There are plenty of people who have brain damage who do not commit crimes and plenty of violent people who have no obvious brain damage.

Nonetheless, 'profiling' quickly became part of the stock of fiction writers, stimulating public fascination with its application to actual cases. By the mid-1990s, journalists would ask of any major police enquiry 'have you brought in a profiler?' Yet, as was mentioned in Chapter 1, the idea that a psychologist can solve a crime by getting into the mind of the criminal is far from reality.

So although the application of psychology to the world of crime has hit the headlines most thoroughly in the idea of 'profiling' serial killers to help the police catch them, this owes more to fiction than to fact. It is not often appreciated that the profilers portrayed in fiction are just contemporary versions of all those imaginary detectives that were inspired by Sherlock Holmes. To make the fiction entertaining, it is essential that these often wayward 'profilers' are portrayed as gifted individuals, whose surprising insights make a crucial, integrated contribution to police investigations, solving the crimes. Yet, the fiction ignores the fact that police investigations are complex unfolding processes that go through many stages. It is rare that knowledge of the character or personality of an unknown offender contributes very much to the solving of a crime.

One of the cases that is much cited as an early illustration of the mastery of offender profiling reveals rather well the fact that it is usually less exciting than is often portrayed. Over 16 years until 1951, homemade bombs were left in public places in New York. The bomber sent letters to newspapers which made clear that he was seeking revenge for 'dastardly acts' committed against him by the Consolidated Edison Company. Unable to locate the person who became known as the 'Mad Bomber', the police sought the help of Dr James Brussel, a New York psychiatrist. He claimed that 'by studying a man's deed, I have deduced what kind of man he might be', so presaging 'offender profiling'.

Brussel gave a detailed account of the likely offender, which included a description of his physique and education and such intriguing details as that he had never progressed past the Oedipal stage of love for his mother, as well as the often-quoted comment that the Mad Bomber would be wearing a buttoned, double-breasted suit when caught. When George Metesky was eventually convicted of the bombings, it was revealed that much of Brussel's description was accurate, down to the fastened, double-breasted suit. Metesky's Oedipal fixation was not really open to test.

Brussel's apparently remarkable predictions were soon heralded as the start of offender profiling and caught the public imagination for what it now seemed a new generation of psychiatric detectives could do. However, on close examination, Brussel's profile does not appear to have contributed to the police investigation and the identification of Metesky at all. The most useful thing that the New York psychiatrist did was to encourage the police to make public the bombings and letters, which they had tried to keep secret. These newspaper reports in their turn led a clerk at Con Edison to look carefully through the files for any employees who had made threats as part of their compensation claims. Metesky's file contained letters that included very similar wording to that in the Mad Bomber's missives.

The fastened, double-breasted suit is also a less impressive prediction when it is realized that most men wore double-breasted suits in those days, and such suits are rarely worn unbuttoned. With hindsight, we can see that the value of Brussel's contribution lay in the guidance he gave to the police about how to open up their investigation, not in his speculations about the bomber's Oedipal problems.

It therefore has to be appreciated that making these profiling inferences about the perpetrator from the information available at the crime scene, or from witnesses or victims, is even more difficult than getting reliable information in the first place. However, since Brussel's first offering, more soundly based processes have emerged, from FBI agents' attempts at generating such 'profiles' on the basis of their personal experiences and insights. A developing science is evolving at the core of investigative psychology which is showing how such inferences can be reliably made. Studies of solved cases are showing that there are recognizable consistencies between what an offender may do when carrying out an arson attack, or a rape of a stranger, or even a burglary, and other aspects of his life that could lead the police to him.

Despite the thrill such 'profiles' can give to fiction, the reality is that the guidance derived from inferences about offenders' characteristics is often rather mundane and relate most usefully to practical suggestions of how the investigation should proceed. This can include what sorts of criminal records should be searched to generate a list of possible offenders, aspects of the skills and social background likely to characterize the offender – which may be useful to the police in searching through possible suspects elicited from other sources, such as house-to-house enquiries, and suggestions about the mental state of the offender and the possibilities of some psychiatric record. Considerations may further be given to how a suspect may best be interviewed on the basis of inferences made from the criminal events.

The essence of producing guidance for detectives is working out the implications of what actually happened in the crime. The central argument is what I call the 'consistency principle'. The actions in a crime will be generally consistent with how the offender acts in non-criminal situations, even though they may be more extreme when part of a crime. A number of pointers have emerged as being useful to consider. They can be couched as five main questions:

1) What does the crime indicate about the intelligence and knowledge of the offender?
2) What does it suggest about his degree of planning or impulsivity?

3) How does the criminal interact with the explicit or implicit victim?
4) What do his actions indicate about the degree of familiarity with the situation or circumstances of the crime?
5) What particular skills does the offender have?

Interestingly, these questions draw attention to aspects of the crime that are usually ignored when considering the general causes of crime. Even within therapeutic settings, working with offenders, the actual details of crimes are not often explored, but rather general personality characteristics of the offender are the focus. If the crime is considered, it may be only through the offender's account of it rather than working with the sort of detailed, objective information the police have.

The psychological autopsy

One rather unusual activity of making inferences about a person occurs when the cause of death is equivocal. This can happen if there is some doubt as to whether a person committed suicide, suffered an accident, or was murdered. In such cases, an attempt may be made to establish the characteristics of the deceased in order to throw light on what happened. It is not the body of the person on which the autopsy is conducted, but his psychology. This can be derived from documents such as letters, diaries, blogs, or emails the deceased has left behind and interviews with all who knew him.

This is not an easy task, especially if suicide is an issue, because the people closely associated with the dead person may feel some guilt if he killed himself and so be keen to establish some untoward circumstance. If a murder enquiry is in progress, there may also be legal hurdles put in the way of interviewing all the people who have some knowledge of the dead person. The prosecution and defence are likely to have access to different sets of witnesses, who may hold opposing views.

One important example of the confusions that can surround inferences about a dead person is the examination of the explosion in the gun turret on the US Navy battleship *USS Ohio* in 1989 which killed 47 of the turret's crewmen. FBI agents carried out what they called an 'equivocal death analysis' of the incident and those in the turret room. This concluded that one of the crew members, Clayton Hartwig, had exploded the gun in an act of suicide. Subsequently, the American Psychological Association set up a special working party to review what the FBI had done and related evidence. They were critical of the FBI report and did not all support the view that Hartig had committed suicide. A further detailed technical examination of the gun concluded that there had been an accidental overram of the gun, which caused it to explode. Subsequent enquiries challenged this conclusion, which shows just how complex the examination of equivocal deaths can be.

Geographical profiling

One particularly useful development within investigative psychology has emerged from the combination of psychological and geographical ways of analysing crime information. This is known as 'geographical offender profiling' (GOP). It is helpful to distinguish the 'decision-support systems' that are central to GOP from 'expert systems'. In the 1990s, there was a fond belief that computers would soon be able to think like people and could be programmed to act as experts that would make decisions instead of the human counterparts they were replacing. This science fiction fantasy was much fuelled by computer engineers, who obtained large research grants to pursue this Holy Grail. Rather quickly it became clear, as many psychologists had predicted, that, except in very special cases, it was not really possible to replicate the thought processes, knowledge, and experience of human experts.

Somewhat more modest – but still extremely useful – computer systems started to surface in the wake of that discovery. These are systems that help the expert to make a more informed decision and are typically known as decision-support systems. Their task is to tidy up the information available and analyse some aspects of it. This helps an expert to see the patterns within that information and draw upon his or her experience and training to make sense of those patterns. Many of us experience the consequences of such systems whenever we are required to give information to check the use of our credit card. The computer system may have picked up that you wish to spend an amount of money that is unusually large for you, or that you are buying something, or purchasing in a location, that is very different from your normal activity. This alerts various people to explore you and your purchase more closely, which is when you are asked questions about your mother's maiden name or your favourite book.

The example of credit card checking is an interesting illustration of a decision-support system because it is based on the idea that people's habits are reasonably consistent. It is therefore well within the capabilities of modern computers to calculate what is the typical range of values, locations, and/or types of purchase for any given person, then to set up alerts if a purchase steps outside those limits. In some countries, notably the USA, these ideas have been taken a step further by the tax-collecting authorities. They have formulae which enable them to calculate what a typical tax return would be for a person in any particular employment. If the return presented is noticeably different from what the formula suggests, then that person's accounts will be very closely scrutinized.

GOP systems work on similar principles to the other decision-support systems mentioned. They are most used when an offender commits a number of crimes, the assumption being that just as we may tend to use a particular range of shops in a given area, so an offender will tend to limit his crimes to a given locality. Of course, not all offenders do this, just as we do not always shop in the same places. But the remarkable finding is that enough offenders are sufficiently consistent in the locations in

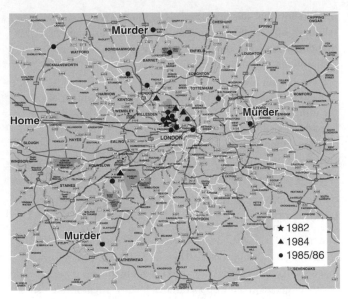

13. A map of the locations of a crime series with the location of the offender's home indicated

which they chose to offend for this to be a useful starting point for trying to work out where the offender lives.

The system moves this basic idea on a couple of steps. Firstly, it is assumed that the further an offender is from home, the less likely he is to commit a crime. Secondly, if the *opportunities* for crimes are relatively evenly distributed around his home, then the crimes themselves are liable to be distributed around his home. The consequence of these two assumptions is that if a series of crimes is known to have been carried out by the same offender, then he is likely to be living within the area those crimes surround. A widely quoted 'circle hypothesis' is drawn to summarize this idea. If a circle is drawn with the diameter being formed by a line joining the two crimes furthest from each other, then the home is likely to be within this circle, probably towards its centre. Remarkably, results show that this hypothesis is supported for the majority of criminals who commit more than five crimes; although of course that does mean that for a large number of offenders these assumptions are not valid at all.

The circle hypothesis is a relatively simple development of the initial assumption. More sophisticated algorithms have been developed that use probability calculations built into decision-support mapping software such as the aptly named Dragnet system. Such software is increasingly being drawn upon by police forces around the world.

Linking crimes

The more information available on an offender, the more readily an investigation can proceed. Therefore, if it can be determined that a set of crimes has all been carried out by the same person, this 'series' offers up greater opportunities for investigators. It also can make the prosecution more powerful through 'similar fact evidence'. If a jury thinks the series of offences is the work of one person, especially in matters that turn on the issue of consent, as in rape, then they are more likely to convict.

Not all crimes can be linked so readily, by witnesses' descriptions, fingerprints, fibres, DNA, or the like. So attempts are made to link them by behavioural means. This is most feasible if there are some behaviours that are very unusual, such as in one case of a series of rapes where the offender gagged the victim by putting his hand forcefully into her mouth. But that does require some knowledge of what the prevalence of various behaviours are in the types of crimes being linked. A subtle set of statistical calculations can therefore be necessary.

Intriguingly, though, with many crimes, their locations are a good indicator of whether they may be the acts of the same person. This is especially true of very rare crimes like the rape of a stranger, but it can also be the case with more common crimes like burglary.

Serial and spree killers, and mass murderers

There is no single pathway along which all offenders travel to become criminals. Furthermore, any one category of offence – such as murder, robbery, or fraud – will also have many variants. Each of these can have quite different precursors. Therefore, any guidance to the police based on assumptions about the characteristics of the offenders has to be derived from aspects that distinguish between crimes. To clarify, I am often asked for the 'profile of a serial killer', but although these vicious, disturbing killers are very rare indeed, they vary considerably. There is no one 'profile' that fits all. That is true for all offenders. We need to consider the details of the crime very carefully in order to try and determine what characterizes any particular offender.

In relation to serial killers, a distinction needs to be drawn between those men (I can think of no women) who kill a number of people in one spree and others who will kill a number of individuals at different points in time. The Columbine School shooters are one widely known example of spree killers, but sadly there continue to be many others who will, typically, shoot a number of people in one outburst. These spree killers almost inevitably end up dead, shot by others during the course of their outrage or shooting themselves at the end of their outburst. Their actions are therefore best thought of as a violent, extravagant form of suicide. They have a lot in common with other people who kill themselves. They feel isolated and often are overtly depressed, but they also rage against others whom they blame for their low self-esteem and who they believe have caused them harm. They want to make a statement and get others to notice. Usually, these 'others' are some generalized group or institution like a school or a fast-food franchise, a company or a community. These killers have much in common with suicide bombers, even though those individuals clothe their anger in ideological rhetoric.

People (typically men, but sometimes women) who kill others over a period of time, with what is often referred to as a 'cooling-off' period between each murder, are a much more varied mix of individuals. Once they have killed three people with some interval between the killings, most experts are willing to call them 'serial killers'. However, under this umbrella term are many different kinds of vicious people. It can include those who are referred to as 'killing for profit'. Many of the best-known examples of this lived in Victorian times and earlier. Perhaps the most gruesome were Burke and Hare who killed people so that they could sell their bodies to the burgeoning schools of anatomy. As I write, a woman in Iran known as Mahin stands accused of killing a number of people who innocently took lifts in her car. She stole their possessions to sell on in order to pay off her debts. As in so many other similar cases, it has to be said that one of the causes of these serial killings is that the murderers find they can get away with their crimes over and over again. As is sometimes said, one of the causes of serial killing is an incompetent police force.

Nevertheless, it is not only cold, calculating killers who, from time to time, seem able to avoid capture over months, and sometimes years. Many ruthless killers seem to be driven by anger or what may even appear to them to be a 'mission'. They typically choose vulnerable victims, such as sex workers who ply their trade on the streets, or people living in shanty towns who are not readily missed. Fred West picked on young women on their own, away from home, whose families had little knowledge of their whereabouts. A very few of these serial killers are mentally disturbed, mutilating the bodies of their victims, finding some bizarre gratification in treating these people as objects. Others are strongly sexually motivated; they rape and abuse the people they entrap and then kill them to avoid detection.

One other group of people are mass murderers. They are even more diverse than serial killers, killing a number of people, not in a violent spree, or over a period of time like serial killers, but as part of some greater atrocity. This would cover various forms of genocide and war crimes. Some authorities would even include the mass suicide in Jonestown in Guyana in 1978, in which 918 people died under the direction of the cult leader Jim Jones. Such considerations, though, take us into state violence and open up moral and legal questions far beyond forensic psychology. But one aspect of this is worthy of some attention here – terrorism.

The challenge of terrorism

Since the attack on the Twin Towers and Pentagon on 11 September 2001, there has been a tremendous increase in interest in terrorism. Central to this is an attempt to make sense of how people can so callously kill others in the name of some abstract ideology. Such outrages have always been with us, from the fight against Roman domination of Judea by Zealots in the 1st century, through to the assassins in the 13th century who were a breakaway faction of Shia Islam, and on to the Fenians in the 19th century who challenged British rule in Ireland, and the terrorist group at the start of the 20th century who contributed to the start of the Great War by murdering Archduke Franz Ferdinand.

Over a hundred years ago, anarchists such as Mikhail Bakunin articulated the concept that underlies most terrorist acts in writing of 'the propaganda of the deed'. This encapsulated the mission of many groups who seek to have an impact on public opinion, and consequently the stability of governments, through attacks on people or buildings that they see as being of political or ideological significance.

Therefore, although it is tempting to classify terrorists with other criminals or search for mental disorder in their backgrounds, the salutary conclusion that must be drawn from many studies is that they are often indistinguishable from other law-abiding citizens, except for their missionary zeal. A high proportion of them are more highly educated than the populous from whom they are drawn. The origin of their commitment to a violent cause therefore has to be found in their associates and experiences.

In drawing attention to the social and cultural context of violence against strangers, we are also alerted to the role that social processes play in all offending activity. There is a temptation for psychologists to see the roots of criminality in the make-up of the person, but the social and cultural origins of crimes should never be ignored. As discussed in Chapter 2, every offence has some explicit or implicit social interaction. These interactions are shaped by the interpersonal context in which the criminal grows and develops. No offence can ever be entirely explained by the characteristics of the individual criminal.

Expanding horizons

Once law-enforcement agencies became aware of the power of scientific psychology, they started to draw on its insights for many areas of their activity. There have been studies as varied as the examination of why people travel over the speed limit in their cars, or what gives rise to police corruption. Those involved in hostage negotiation, or talking to those who are threatening to kill themselves, now expect to have some background introduction at least to major issues in forensic psychology and the psychology of persuasion. Police officers working undercover may be given psychological help when they need to surface back into the law-abiding community.

Particularly important, also, has been a change in attitudes towards, and management of, the trauma that police officers may suffer as part of their work. In the past, there would be a bar in the police headquarters, and traumatized police officers would be expected to be 'manly' and not talk about what they had suffered but drown it in drink. No wonder, then, that so many marriages were ruined and these men were broken people by the time they retired. Nowadays, many law-enforcement agencies will expect to have a confidential counselling service that is freely available to everyone they employ. This is recognition, to quote the Gilbert and Sullivan song, that the policeman's lot is often not a happy one.

There are great pressures involved in most investigations, and much of police activity does itself merge into counselling or other forms of psychological support or intervention. Hostage and barricade incidents are a particular example where a police officer who does not understand the psychological issues involved can make a difficult situation worse. Crowd control or dealing with traffic accidents are other potentially stressful situations. The pressures on the police can also come from contact with criminals, especially in the context of undercover operations. Therefore an understanding of these pressures can help to prevent police corruption.

Most of these contributions draw on organizational and social psychology. They have much in common with the issues faced in most organizations, but especially those that have to deal with distress and the suffering of others. The selection of people who will be able to withstand the pressures of the job and effective ways of managing people under stressful conditions are consequently increasingly influenced by what psychologists have learned in many other settings. Sadly, though, it is still rare for police officers or those in many other law-enforcement agencies to have the basic grounding in psychology to be able to make really effective use of all that the discipline has to offer them.

Conclusions

Psychologists are contributing to all stages of the investigative process, including the important stages before the investigation, in helping to select police officers. They are helping to set up effective systems for collecting and making sense of all the information needed during an inquiry. This includes detailed consideration of the crucial processes of interviewing witnesses, victims, or suspects.

Clues are usually thought of as strands of twine that if carefully followed will eventually lead to the culprit. They may be as varied as a footprint left at the scene of the crime, or a particular way of breaking into a house, or even something that did not happen, as in fictional cases where dogs do not bark, thus indicating they probably knew the intruder. But what has caught the public imagination for the last quarter of a century has been the possibility that something rather more intangible, like the style of an offence, could act as a clue. Such clues would not only lead to the identity of the culprit but could reveal something of his or her personality. This became known as 'offender profiling'.

In practice, the contributions from psychology to inferences about an offender, from details of the crime, have been far less dramatic than fictional accounts indicate. Nonetheless, the utility of these psychological inputs has been great enough to open the way to the new area of investigative psychology. This covers ways of improving the quality of testimony, including approaches to the detection of deception, methods of managing police data, linking crimes to a common offender, as well as a broad range of inputs to the management of police enquiries. Offender profiling is a part of all this, but as time goes on it takes an ever less prominent role.

Chapter 7
Always the bridesmaid?

One intriguing aspect of forensic psychology emerges from the canter (pun intended) through the field covered in previous chapters. Forensic psychologists tend to be advisers in territories that are defined as being the domain of one or more other professions. They may be helping detectives carrying out investigations, giving guidance to lawyers on how to prepare a case for court, or offering opinions to judges and juries. They may be working in prisons or with probation officers, in special hospitals for mentally ill offenders overseen by a psychiatrist, or involved in various community projects led by social workers, psychiatric nurses, or civil servants. It is as if their role is nearly always a supportive one, like that of a bridesmaid seldom in the central position of the bride.

This situation will probably not be the dominant one for much longer because the exploding interest in forensic psychology is drawing ever more capable people into this area. Around the world, it is the most rapidly developing area of professional psychology. This has an interesting consequence: there are more and more well-qualified people applying for employment in forensic psychology. Selection processes will tend to choose the most able, so the effectiveness of the people in these jobs is growing all the time. As happened in areas of professional psychology that emerged in earlier decades, notably in the organizational, educational, and clinical domains, positions that started off merely as assessors who were adjunct to the main players soon took on managerial and other leadership roles. In these new roles, the impact of a scientific psychology, with its standardized tests and experimental methods, developing theories and objective procedures, was able to demonstrate its power.

The crucial foundation of all this is a tradition of careful research. It is probably in this more academic arena that forensic psychologists are starting to lead the way. To do this, they have had to shake off the shackles of a strongly clinical tradition. For an older generation, this has been difficult, but younger researchers do not see themselves as footnotes to clinical psychology and are ready and able to draw on the full range of the psychological and behavioural sciences.

The increasing professionalization of forensic psychology is also giving more power to its elbow. A quarter of a century ago, anyone with some background in psychology could drift into a forensic context and offer up guidance. The term 'forensic psychologist' itself, however, tended to be limited to people who had a clinical psychology background, working with patients who had found their way to them through the courts. These traditions still exist in some places, but in English-speaking countries there has been a strong growth in the establishment of distinct professional divisions for forensic psychologists.

This is illustrated in the UK by the term 'chartered forensic psychologist' being controlled by law. In order to be allowed to use this title, you must first obtain a degree in psychology that is recognized by the British Psychological Society. Then a specific, accredited, twelve-months' Master's programme must be completed. Finally, you must work for two years in practice, supervised by a person who already has chartered status. This is a minimum of a six-year training period, equivalent to most other professions.

Unfinished business

Against this exponential growth of forensic psychology has to be set the large number of topics that are still hardly touched upon but to which the discipline can without doubt contribute. Such topics can be found in each of the settings we have explored in previous chapters.

In relation to courts, there is a growing involvement of psychologists in civil proceedings. This can be dealing with disputed documents or challenges to the sanity of people who have written contested wills. Some of this overlaps with the work of linguists, but in other cases, especially in the family courts, the assessment of the individuals in dispute can benefit considerably from psychological input, but the scientific basis for the psychologists' activities still needs much development.

Work with offenders is growing apace as prison psychologists become an ever more integrated and respected part of custodial systems. A burgeoning area of forensic psychology is helping offenders whose sentences do not include imprisonment, or once they emerge from these institutions. However, as we have noted is often the case, the psychologist's role is still often merely supportive, limiting their potential influence.

The new area of investigative psychology is probably the one with the greatest number of new questions waiting for detailed study. To pick just a few, these include:

- Why do people give false alibis to support people they know are criminal?
- What is the process by which offenders are willing to make false appeals, asking for help in finding a missing loved one, whom they have killed?
- What is the most effective way to manage angry crowds?
- What psychological pathways lead people into terrorism?

14. Murder can have a shattering impact on the whole community, as these memorials to the victims of Mark Dutroux testify

Forensic psychology is broadening its range and grasp at a rate that some people may consider alarming. Initially, most psychology of crime dealt with extreme crime of a highly emotional nature that related to obvious mental problems. But now what are known as 'volume crimes', such as burglary and theft, are coming into the remit of psychologists. The potential here is enormous, given that only around one out of every ten of such crimes are solved.

The criminal courts were also the dominant domain of psychological experts, but increasingly they are finding their way into family courts and a widening range of civil proceedings. Some experts in the USA are even providing evidence in support of claims of negligence by large companies, such as those managing shopping malls. These claims are brought by victims of crime who seek redress on the grounds that the shopping mall facilitated certain sorts of criminal acts.

Crime does not stand still. It has an almost ecological capability of evolving to fill any niche that provides an opportunity. Therefore, new technologies and globalization are generating new forms of crime such as cybercrime and international terrorism. One important question is whether this is drawing different sorts of people into crime or are those who would be criminal anyway just changing how they offend? These crimes provide a profound challenge for developed nations and therefore are areas in which psychologists are attempting to make some contribution.

Policy implications

Unlike many areas of psychology, forensic psychology almost inevitably carries policy, ethical, and legal implications. Yet at present the voices of psychologists are not listened to with much interest in the ancient corridors of power, such as parliaments and high courts of justice. This may be in part because the scientific discipline in which psychologists are schooled tends to underplay the importance of values and the societal implications of their 'discoveries'.

One illustration of how fraught such considerations can be is the general utilization of 'profiles' of potential offenders in stop and search or airport security checks. The simple statistics will demonstrate that if people of type X are examined more frequently than people of type Y, then a higher proportion of X people will be found guilty in some way. This thereby increases the belief that the profile of type X is useful for such checks, and a vicious cycle is set in motion. Psychologists should be aware of these issues. They are in a position to be open in explaining them and helping to set up procedures that will militate against the destructive effects that can be caused by the self-fulfilling prophecy and the naïve use of such predictive techniques.

At the even more general level, psychologists have been relatively quiet about the processes that will help to reduce crime. They have concentrated on assisting in catching and convicting people, or providing ways of helping them once convicted, but there needs to be more psychological discussion of whether crime prevention is solely a social, economic, or political matter.

Further reading

New general textbooks on forensic psychology seem to emerge every few months. Therefore to get a more detailed, up-to-date overview of this rapidly developing field, it is best to seek out the most recent books. However, at the time of writing, the following can be recommended:

C. R. Bartol and A. M. Bartol, *Introduction to Forensic Psychology: Research and Application* (London: Sage, 2008)

D. Canter and D. Youngs, *Investigative Psychology: Offender Profiling and the Analysis of Criminal Action* (Chichester: Wiley, 2009)

D. A. Crighton and G. J. Towl, *Psychology in Prisons*, 2nd edn. (Oxford: BPS Blackwell, 2008)

D. Howitt, *Introduction to Forensic and Criminal Psychology* (London: Prenice Hall, 2009)

M. T. Huss, *Forensic Psychology: Research, Clinical Practice, and Applications* (Chichester: Wiley-Blackwell, 2009)

D. A. Kraus and J. D. Lieberman (eds.), *Psychological Expertise in Court* (Farnham: Ashgate, 2009)

J. D. Lieberman and D. A. Kraus (eds.), *Jury Psychology: Social Aspects of the Trial Process* (Farnham: Ashgate, 2009)

A. Vrij, *Detecting Lies and Deceit: Pitfalls and Opportunities* (Chichester: Wiley, 2008)

Useful websites

http://www.bps.org.uk/dfp/. This is the site for the Forensic Psychology division of the British Psychological Society, particularly useful for career information.

http://www.all-about-forensic-psychology.com. A site that covers an
exhaustive amount of information.

http://www.ia-ip.org. The International Academy of Investigative
Psychology site.

http://www.davidcanter.com. If you want to know more about the
author of this book.

Glossary

actus reus: that a criminal act has occurred (literally, 'guilty act')

adversarial court system: frequently referred to as 'accusatorial', a court system in which each side presents a case (prosecution and defence) before a court

algorithm: a mathematical procedure that follows a specific sequence

antisocial personality disorder: a mental illness that is listed in the DSM that is characterized by antisocial behaviour

automatism: a criminal defence that claims a defendant's actions are automatic or involuntary

civil cases: cases that are concerned with private rights, as disputes between two individuals

clinical psychology: a branch of psychology focusing on the assessment and treatment of mental disorders and cognitive and behavioural problems

criteria-based content analysis (CBCA): method of analysing statements in terms of indices that are believed to reflect truthfulness

DNA: deoxyribonucleic acid – the material inside the nucleus of cells that carries genetic information that is unique to each individual

expert evidence: contribution made by a person employed to give evidence on a subject who by training, knowledge, and experience is qualified to express a professional opinion

false confession: any confession or admission to a criminal act that the confessor did not commit

guilty knowledge test (GKT): a method of detecting guilt or innocence in which suspects are asked to respond to questions for which only a guilty person is expected to know the correct alternative answer. The guilty subject should experience more physiological arousal to the correct alternative compared to the others, while an innocent suspect will react similarly to all alternatives

instrumental violence: violence committed with a purpose, or in a planned or organized manner

jurisdiction: the authority of a court in any particular location

mens rea: there is criminal intent/responsibility (literally, 'guilty mind')

post-traumatic stress disorder: an anxiety disorder precipitated by a traumatic event that leads to symptoms involving re-experiencing the event, avoidance of event-related stimuli, and increased arousal

projective test: a personality test that involves the presentation of ambiguous stimuli

psychopathy: a clinical term to describe deficits in interpersonal and emotional functioning

recidivism: repeat criminal behaviour, normally defined by an additional criminal conviction

reliability: a statistical term related to the consistency and stability of measurement

risk assessment: procedures for estimating the likelihood of future offending by an individual

risk management: procedures to contain or reduce the likelihood of recurrence of harmful behaviour

sentence: the penalty imposed on an individual found guilty of an offence in a court of law

statement validity analysis (SVA): a method of assessing the veracity of witness statements by considering specific details of what is reported

structured professional judgement: a form of assessment in which the assessor uses a structured risk-assessment tool

suggestibility: the degree to which an individual may be unduly influenced by forms of questioning or the power of the questioner

syndrome evidence: evidence that refers to a set of symptoms occurring together in a meaningful manner

trauma: a powerful, disturbing experience that may have long-lasting effects

ultimate issue testimony: expert testimony in which the expert gives a conclusion that answers the question that is presently before the court

validity: the extent to which a measurement measures what it claims to measure

voice stress analysis: a technique that claims to detect lying by measuring variations in the physical properties of sounds made when speaking

weapon focus: paying attention to a threat from a weapon to the detriment of noting the appearance of the offender

Index

Index

CLASSICS
A Very Short Introduction
Mary Beard and John Henderson

This Very Short Introduction to Classics links a haunting temple on a lonely mountainside to the glory of ancient Greece and the grandeur of Rome, and to Classics within modern culture – from Jefferson and Byron to Asterix and Ben-Hur.

'The authors show us that Classics is a "modern" and sexy subject. They succeed brilliantly in this regard ... nobody could fail to be informed and entertained – and the accent of the book is provocative and stimulating.'

John Godwin, *Times Literary Supplement*

'Statues and slavery, temples and tragedies, museum, marbles, and mythology – this provocative guide to the Classics demystifies its varied subject-matter while seducing the reader with the obvious enthusiasm and pleasure which mark its writing.'

Edith Hall

www.oup.co.uk/vsi/classics